Davies and Penhall's
Sunny Afternoon

W0114813

'They make the Rolling Stones look like US Marines'

— police officer

When 'You Really Got Me' exploded on Swinging London in 1964, the Kinks forever changed the course of rock 'n' roll. Ray Davies and Joe Penhall's Olivier Award-winning *Sunny Afternoon* (2014) covers the band's formative years of 1964–7, when four working-class North London lads broke through to become one of the most unlikely and influential rock bands of the 1960s. Mixing the comic adventures of 'Dave the Rave' with the touching introspection of Ray's some-times fragile psyche, Joe Penhall's script weaves Ray Davies' songs, both the hits and lesser-known works, into one of the finest jukebox musicals of the new millennium.

Drawing on a wealth of background material, John Fleming examines the blend of events and songs selected, reconsidering the relationship between biography and drama to shed new light on the Kinks and the musical that tells their story.

John Fleming is Dean of the College of Fine Arts and Communication at Texas State University.

The Fourth Wall

The Fourth Wall series is a growing collection of short books on famous plays. Its compact format perfectly suits the kind of fresh, engaging criticism that brings a play to life.

Each book in this series selects one play or musical as its subject and approaches it from an original angle, seeking to shed light on an old favourite or break new ground on a modern classic. These lively, digestible books are a must for anyone looking for new ideas on the major works of modern theatre.

Also available in this series:

Coming soon:

Davies and Penhall's
Sunny Afternoon

John Fleming

LONDON AND NEW YORK

First published 2017
by Routledge
2 Park Square, Milton Park, Abingdon, Oxon OX14 4RN

and by Routledge
711 Third Avenue, New York, NY 10017

Routledge is an imprint of the Taylor & Francis Group, an informa business

© 2017 John Fleming

The right of John Fleming to be identified as author of this
work has been asserted by him in accordance with sections 77
and 78 of the Copyright, Designs and Patents Act 1988.

British Library Cataloguing-in-Publication Data
A catalogue record for this book is available from
the British Library

Library of Congress Cataloguing-in-Publication Data
Names: Fleming, John (Author)
Title: Davies and Penhall's Sunny afternoon / John Fleming.
Description: Abingdon, Oxon; New York, NY : Routledge, 2017. |
Series: The fourth wall | Includes bibliographical references.
Identifiers: LCCN 2016057692| ISBN 9781138239944 (pbk.) |
ISBN 9781315294698 (ebook)
Subjects: LCSH: Davies, Ray, 1944– Sunny Afternoon. |
Kinks (Musical group)
Classification: LCC ML420.D25 F54 2017 |
DDC 782.42166092–dc23 LC record available at
https://lccn.loc.gov/2016057692

ISBN: 9781138239944 (pbk)
ISBN: 9781315294698 (ebk)

Typeset in Bembo
by Out of House Publishing

Contents

Introduction

When 'You Really Got Me' exploded on Swinging London in 1964, the Kinks forever changed the course of rock 'n' roll. Led by singer-songwriter Ray Davies and the manic guitar playing of younger brother Dave, the Kinks were in their teens and early twenties when they created some of the most unforgettable songs of the British Invasion. Featuring hits such as 'Waterloo Sunset', 'Lola', 'A Well Respected Man', 'Dedicated Follower of Fashion', the genre-changing power-chord sonic thumpers 'You Really Got Me' and 'All Day and All of the Night', as well as the sing-along title track that defined England's glorious summer of 1966, the Olivier Award-winning *Sunny Afternoon* covers the band's formative years of 1964–7, when four working-class North London lads broke through to become one of the most unlikely and influential rock bands of the 1960s.

With the story directly from Ray Davies, this musical provides an inside look at the formation of the iconic rock band. It chronicles the obstacles the band faced, including numerous financial and contractual disputes with their management and publishing team, a disastrous 1965 US tour that led to a four-year ban from the country, as well as the legendary infighting among the four bandmates. Mixing the comic adventures of 'Dave the Rave' with the touching introspection of Ray's sometimes fragile psyche, Joe Penhall's script weaves Ray Davies' songs, both the hits and lesser-known works, into one of the finest jukebox musicals of the new millennium, a show hailed as the best rock musical since *Jersey Boys* and the best British musical since *Billy Elliot* (2005). Via the collaboration of Davies and Penhall, *Sunny Afternoon* reveals the inner dynamics of the Kinks, while also providing insight on an era that continues to reverberate through popular culture.

Jukebox (or catalogue) musicals use previously released popular songs, typically from a particular singer or group. Some are presented in a revue style while most contextualize the songs into a dramatic plot, which may or may not revolve around the particular group. While jukebox musicals have existed for many years (*Buddy – The Buddy Holly Story* ran in London from 1989 to 2002), it was the success of *Mamma Mia!* (London 1999, Broadway 2001) that spurred the jukebox wave of the new millennium. Based on the music of the Swedish pop group ABBA, *Mamma Mia!* exemplifies the approach of creating a fictional story to fit the songs. In contrast, *Sunny Afternoon* more closely follows the model of *Jersey Boys* (Broadway 2005, London 2008), a show based on the music and lives of Frankie Valli and the Four Seasons. Whereas *Jersey Boys* is structured in four parts, each narrated by a different band member who has his own (often contradictory) perspective on the band, *Sunny Afternoon* is a straightforward narrative, and since the show's story and initial script were developed by Ray Davies, it is his perspective that informs the stage action. (As discussed later, there are moments where Dave Davies has a different recollection of events.)

While Ray Davies is best known for his work with the Kinks, *Sunny Afternoon* marks his fourth foray into musical theatre. While still with the band, he worked on *Chorus Girls* (1981, co-written with Barrie Keefe) and *80 Days* (1988, book by Snoo Wilson). After the Kinks' sudden 1996 demise, Davies intermittently tried to recast his past in theatrical terms, first with his multi-year solo tour *The Storyteller* (which included readings from his 'unauthorized autobiography' *X-Ray*) and then more overtly with *Come Dancing* (written 1997, produced 2008, book co-written with Paul Sirett), a stage musical in which Davies served as the narrator and which was inspired by his sister Rene and the Kinks' hit single of the same name. Davies began writing *Sunny Afternoon* in 2005. While Davies once considered premiering *Sunny Afternoon* in New York, as a songwriter whose work has often been quintessentially British, he eventually realized London was the appropriate place for its premiere.

As with most musicals, the path to first production was a multi-year process marked by pivotal steps that morphed the original idea into its final stage incarnation. It was a suggestion by acclaimed playwright Tom Stoppard to Ray Davies' manager Deke Arlon that brought West End producer Sonia Friedman (who has enjoyed a myriad of successes developing both new plays and new musicals) to the project. In turn, when Davies asked for a playwright as collaborator, Friedman suggested Penhall, and so the two writers began work in 2011, with *Sunny Afternoon* now an official commission of Sonia Friedman Productions. In an interview with Will Mortimer, Penhall detailed the process:

> Once I'd written the first draft of the book I cast actors [including Dagleish and Maguire], a choreographer and

musicians were hired, and I directed two workshops, starting in 2012, with Ray arranging the music. Then Ed [Hall] came on board and directed a third workshop, with the same personnel, freeing me up to concentrate on revisions, and I was able to write key new scenes and complete it.

(Mortimer, 2014)

Penhall also relates the give and take between himself and Davies, as well as a pivotal discovery:

I knew the songs I wanted to use, but [Davies] pointed me in the direction of one or two that I wasn't aware of and I talked him into using songs most people don't know. In the last week of the last workshop it wasn't quite finished, something was missing. I took [Davies] into a room with a piano, locked the door and he told me the story of his big sister Rene, who had died tragically young. What he said was so mesmeric, I simply wrote it down and twenty minutes later John Dagleish was saying the lines. There was a hush in the room. It was like digging up a gold nugget and thrusting it into the light.

(Mortimer, 2014)

As discussed later, that story of how Rene's death influenced Davies serves as the emotional lynchpin of Act One.

While Penhall was crucial to shaping the narrative, the addition of Edward Hall brought both a directorial vision and a venue. As Artistic Director of the Hampstead Theatre, Hall had been looking for a new musical, and after that third workshop, Hall knew he had found the perfect piece. In December 2013 it was announced that *Sunny Afternoon* would premiere at the Hampstead Theatre. Founded in 1959, the Hampstead Theatre has long been known for fostering new work, but the 2014 production of *Sunny Afternoon* marked its first foray into musical theatre. While Davies' music is exceptional, there is also no doubt that the theatrical talents of Joe Penhall (Book), Edward Hall (Director), Elliott Ware (Musical Director), Adam Cooper (Choreography), and Miriam Buether (Designer) were pivotal to *Sunny Afternoon*'s success. Indeed, the Hampstead production was an unqualified hit, earning multiple four- and five-star reviews.

Evening Standard critic Henry Hitchings called the show 'irresistible', noting how it celebrated 'the off-kilter humour and wry pathos of the band's greatest hits', while being a musical with 'deliberate roughness' that 'puts heart and soul above the polished slickness we now tend to associate with celebrity' (Hitchings, 2014). *Daily Telegraph* critic Charles Spencer was equally effusive, calling the show 'wonderful', with Edward Hall's direction 'marvellously nail[ing] the humour and pathos of the piece'. Spencer also cited Davies' theatrical sensibilities, saying his songs 'belong in the pantheon of popular music alongside those of Noel Coward and Cole Porter and are often blessed with a similar mixture of melancholy and wit'. He closed the review by calling *Sunny Afternoon* 'an irresistibly enjoyable and touching night' (Spencer, 2014). *Daily Mail* critic Quentin Letts praised the show for having 'a strong sense of period … [with] well-drawn characters that evolve with the band'. He aptly noted: 'Funny, stylish, well-performed, quirky – it has everything The Kinks had' (Letts, 2014). Likewise, in *The Times*, Dominic Maxwell hailed it as 'the most exhilarating rock 'n' roll stage show since *Jersey Boys*, fuelled by wit, deft storytelling, great acting and musicianship and some of the best pop songs … This is a great, very British musical about a great, very British band' (Maxwell, 2014).

Multiple critics noted that many of the show's highlights can be found in unexpected places, such as the a cappella rendition of 'Days' delivered by their upper-class managers Robert Wace and Grenville Collins, or the moving duet 'when Ray, lost and lonely in America, sings "Sitting in My Hotel" down the line to his young wife Rasa back home in North London, and she answers with "I Go To Sleep", the ballad Ray wrote while worriedly waiting for news of their daughter Louisa's birth' (Halstead, 2014). These moments highlight both the beauty of the show's orchestrations and the ways Davies' songs lend themselves to the storytelling nature of theatre.

Multiple reviewers also highlighted the rich theatricality of Hall's staging, most notably when Dave Davies 'swings from a hotel chandelier dressed only in ladies' lingerie, and a glowing rendition of 'Sunny Afternoon' that summons up the euphoria of England's 1966 World Cup triumph' (Hemming, 2014) complete with Union Jack confetti cascading down upon the theatre audience. Likewise, critics noted the theatrical coup of the show's ending that cleverly mimics a rock concert's encore and which has the audience on its feet clapping and singing to a medley of hits built around the chart-topping 'Lola'.

Designer Miriam Buether also earned accolades for her backdrop of loudspeakers that evoked the aura of a recording studio, but which also featured a centre walkway (reminiscent of the stage set-up the Kinks used in their arena rock shows of the 1980s) and side aisle entrances that fostered performer-audience interaction akin to a concert. Reviewers also noted the eye candy of Buether's costumes for the Davies sisters/dolly birds who wore 'those singularly-of-the-period long white skater boots with knickers that match their bum-skimming frocks' (Clapp, 2014) as they danced on stage and on the walkways, mimicking the moves found on *Top of the Pops* and other shows of the era.

The versatile cast of fifteen, accompanied by two extra musicians, earned universal praise for their acting, singing, and musicianship. Virtually every review highlighted the extraordinary work of Dagleish and Maguire. Dagleish was cited for 'capturing [Ray Davies'] quirkiness and charisma' (Hitchings, 2014) as well as his 'wry, witty grin and underlying sadness' (Spencer, 2014), and for being 'exceptionally good', particularly in his ability to convey 'the idea of Davies as an unusual, brooding creator, the off-beat, stammering Muswell Hill lad who found he was best able to express himself on a guitar' (Letts, 2014). In turn, Maguire was cited for capturing the 'exciting wildness' (Hitchings, 2014) of Dave as he 'plays guitar and sings with brash exuberance' (Maxwell, 2014), and ultimately portrays 'the essence of the younger Davies in his prime' (Halstead, 2014).

The Hampstead reviews clearly indicated the viability of a West End production, and as a subsidiary of the Ambassador Theatre Group, Friedman Productions lined up the intimate Harold Pinter Theatre, which was slightly modified to allow for some cabaret tables in the audience as well as a centre walkway that cut through the first seven rows. The show again earned mostly first-rate reviews, capped by its winning four Olivier Awards, including Best Musical as well as individual awards for Davies, Dagleish, and Maguire.

To provide a closer look at *Sunny Afternoon*, subsequent chapters examine the key players (both the historical figures covered in the show as well as the major theatre artists), the content of Act One, the content of Act Two, and then two appendices: one that provides a *Sunny Afternoon* fact sheet of dates, credits, and awards, and a second that chronicles background information on the show's twenty-eight songs. In the process, these chapters unveil the meaning behind Penhall's apt sentiment: 'I told Ray, "Never let the facts get in the way of a good story." So there's a little poetic licence, but not much' (Mortimer, 2014). As the ensuing chapters show, *Sunny Afternoon* is not only a compendium of Ray Davies' songwriting excellence, it is indeed a good story, the combustible tale of the Kinks with all their inner turmoil and creative genius on display.

The principal players

Since *Sunny Afternoon* is based on actual people, this chapter examines the key figures portrayed in the musical as well as the show's creative team. In the process it provides a broader context for understanding the piece, including an extension of the historical lives beyond the scope of the musical as well as a consideration of why this creative team had the appropriate background for making the show such a success. The presentation examines the Kinks, both as a group and as individuals, their management team, and also *Sunny Afternoon*'s creative team.

The Davies family and the beginnings of the Kinks

The action of *Sunny Afternoon* begins at a point when Ray and Dave were still living at home. As supporting characters, the parents and siblings are presented in bold strokes, and so a brief family history provides a greater sense of the role they played in shaping the Davies brothers path to the musical success depicted in the show.

The children of Fred and Annie Davies, Ray and Dave were the products of a large working-class family, with a

strong influence exerted by the six older sisters. Rose was
born in 1924, followed by Rene (1926), Dolly (1928), Joyce
(1930), Peggy (1932), and Gwen (1938). (Though it is difficult to distinguish them as individuals, the latter three are
named in the West End programme, while a fourth, presum-
ably Dolly, also appears on stage.) Beyond being the only
boys, Ray (21 June 1944) and Dave (3 February 1947) were
the babies of the family, crowded into a small house at
6 Denmark Terrace in Muswell Hill, North London. For
much of his adolescence Ray lived with Rosie, her hus-
band Arthur and their son Terry; likewise, Dave was partly
raised by Dolly. Ultimately, it was a shared love of music
that brought the brothers together. In the early days of the
band, 'The house was so crowded that Ray and Dave slept
in the front room, with their amps under the bed and gear
all around them' (Hasted, 2013: 4). In Kinks lore, that front
room has taken on mythical connotations as the space that
fostered the Davies brothers' love of music. The Saturday
night parties featured his parents' music hall favourites,
while on other occasions the sisters danced and played
piano and banjo in the front room or listened to jazz, big
bands, crooners, country, and early rock 'n' roll. Eventually,
it was in that front room where the Kinks' first hits were
written.

In addition to financial difficulties, the family endured its
share of hardships. As revealed in *Sunny Afternoon*, Rene gave
Ray his first guitar for his thirteenth birthday, and then died
later that night in a dancehall. After Rene's death he was sent
to a child psychiatrist. In Davies' words:

> It was just a counsellor, just a child who was a little but
> troubled, and didn't know how to fit in. More than

anything else, I didn't know how to communicate. That was something with music that helped me later.

(Hasted, 2013: 9)

In the end, it was music that paved the way out for the brothers. Never one for school, Dave got his first guitar when he was twelve. By the time Dave was fourteen, he and Ray were performing instrumental duets for family and friends as well as in the pub across the street, the Clissold Arms; by late 1961, Peter Quaife had joined them, and they were playing local halls and school dances (Dave Davies, 1996: 19). The nascent band went through various names (the Ray Davies Quartet (or RDQ), the Ramrods, the Boll Weevils, and the Ravens) and drummers (John Start, then Micky Willett); along the way Ray also branched out, playing with the Dave Hunt Rhythm and Blues Band and Hamilton King's Blues Messengers band. In January 1964, the Ravens changed their name to the Kinks; that same month, the band's first official recording session occurred at Pye Studios. That day they recorded four songs, including a cover version of 'Long Tall Sally' and three songs by Ray: 'I Took My Baby Home', 'You Do Something to Me', and 'You Still Want Me'. These would be the A and B sides to their first two singles; 'Sally' briefly charted at #42, while 'Do Something' sank without a trace. Since the original contract was for three singles, when they went to record 'You Really Got Me' it was truly a make or break proposition.

The band

While the Davies brothers are the best-known members of the Kinks, Pete Quaife and Mick Avory were pivotal to the band's early sound and success. While *Sunny Afternoon* makes some direct reference to aspects of their lives, it also includes subtle details that convey unstated attributes of the rhythm section and the ways they contributed to the band's chemistry. In fact, purists such as film and video director Julien Temple believe the Kinks 'were never the same after Quaife left, let alone following Avory's departure' (Rogan, 2015: 637).

Pete Quaife (31 December 1943–23 June 2010) was a founding member, bass guitarist, and backing vocalist for the Kinks. Born in Tavistock, Devon, his family later moved to the Muswell Hill area where he attended William Grimshaw secondary school with Ray and Dave; he also briefly attended Hornsey Art College with Ray and worked in the commercial art world. Described as 'a sardonically funny extrovert' and 'a daring, hip dresser' (Hasted, 2013:12), Quaife was the Mod member of the group who enjoyed exploring the fashion scene of Carnaby Street. While often overshadowed by the Davies brothers, he initially did a fair amount of press for the band and was known as being the peacemaker. Severely injured in a car accident, Quaife took a medical leave from the band in June 1966, then quit in September, only to return in November. In early 1969, during rehearsals for *Arthur (Or the Decline and Fall of the British Empire)*, Quaife permanently left the band. In later interviews he cited the continual fighting, the (then) dearth of touring, and the lack of creative input as reasons for his departure. After a brief stint with a band called Mapleoak, he left the music business in 1970. In a 1996 *Goldmine* magazine interview, the Who's John Entwistle provided a perspective on Quaife's sometimes unacknowledged expertise/contribution: 'I'd say one of my favorite bass players was Pete Quaife because he literally drove the Kinks along.'

Mick Avory (15 February 1944) was the final one to join the Kinks. Born in East Moseley, Surrey, Avory is the only member who grew up outside the Muswell Hill area. He played for a variety of bands including 'in the summer of 1962, playing in [or at least rehearsing with] an early, unnamed incarnation of the Rolling Stones with Brian Jones and Mick Jagger' (Jovanovic, 2013: 59). According to Avory, the idea of being a full-time drummer was 'a bit precarious' and not 'a good industry for regular work' (Jovanovic, 2013: 59). In January 1964, after a string of manual labour jobs, Avory was ready to pursue music as more than just a weekend gig, and so when the Kinks, who had just recorded their first single, asked him to be their drummer, he quit his paraffin delivery job.

For the first year, Avory played the live shows, but producer Shel Talmy often hired session drummers for studio recordings, including 'You Really Got Me'. Drumming-wise, Avory had jazz-oriented inclinations, and in retrospect Ray often attributed Mick as providing 'those happy mistakes, those errors that make a band unique' (Ray Davies, 2013: 28). In the early rhythm section 'Avory seemed to slot into Pete Quaife, who had a certain flair on the bass' (Ray Davies, 2013: 28). In band disputes, Avory often sided with Ray over Dave, and by 1984 the fissure between Mick and Dave resulted in Avory leaving the band; however, he stayed on to manage Konk Studios, the recording studio the Kinks created and where the Kinks recorded all their albums from 1973 through to their demise. Since the 1990s, Avory has performed with numerous bands, including the Kast Off Kinks (comprised primarily of former Kinks members) as well as various groups that feature other rock musicians who got their start in the 1960s.

The management team

A central plot point of *Sunny Afternoon* revolves around the band's dispute with management. While some critics viewed it as almost a cliché, the conflict with management is not simply a stage device, but rather was a stark reality. The conflict's roots can be found in the particular biographies of the management team, with the amateurs Wace and Collins ill-prepared to deal with the experienced Page and Kassner, individuals who knew how to capitalize on the situation. It would require Allen Klein's forceful personality to resolve the management dispute.

Robert Wace, along with Collins, formed the early management team for the band. An upper-class product of old money, Wace was well-spoken, well-educated, and moved in very different social circles than the Davies brothers. Well over six feet tall, with a plummy voice, Wace met Mickey Willet, the then-drummer for the Boll Weevils, and they hatched the unlikely plan of working together; at a handful of gigs on the debutante circuit, Wace sang lead vocals, while the Boll Weevils served as his backing band. When they branched out of the society circles and played a club in East London, Wace was booed off stage and abandoned his singing career. Though only in their very early twenties with no experience in the music business, Wace and Collins were asked to stay on as the band's managers. Wace formally left his father's company and devoted his time to managing the band, a task he enjoyed until the end of 1971, when, after being asked to take a cut in management fee, he angrily resigned.

Grenville Collins was a stockbroker, but like his friend Wace, he longed for something more exciting than his middle-class career path. Jovanovic reports that initially

Collins 'continued to work the stock market, [and] agreed to make 50 per cent of his annual profits available to the venture in return for a percentage of the group's earnings' (Jovanovic, 2013: 45). While the band retrospectively lament their managers' lack of music business acumen, there were times their professionalism and social sensibilities came in handy, such as when Collins rescued a violent, belligerent Dave from a Copenhagen jail following a riot at a 1965 concert; Collins needed to take control because the Kinks were performing later that night in London at the *NME* Pollwinners Party, where they were the closing act, playing after the Beatles (Hasted, 2013: 39–40). While Wace and Collins' failure to accompany the band on their first American tour proved disastrous, their company Boscobel Productions Ltd served as the driving force to recruit Allen Klein, find a new publisher (Freddy Bienstock, head of Belinda Music), and break the contract with Page and Kassner. Ultimately, Collins stayed with the band until 1971; after the Kinks signed a new record deal with RCA, Collins amicably resigned and left the music business.

Forever linked as the unlikely duo managing the Kinks at their breakthrough, Wace and Collins shared many similarities, but also a few differences, with Avory stating: 'Robert was funny because he did upper-class twit things. Grenville was really funny, a hooray Henry sort of bloke who came out with great one-liners. [Though both were about 6'5"] Robert was very thin, whereas everything was big about Grenville' (Hasted, 2013: 77). One can hear Collins' voice on 1966's *Face to Face* where he delivers the voice introduction ('Hello, who's that speaking, please?') to the song 'Party Line'.

Larry Page (born Leonard Davis, 1938–) came aboard after Wace and Collins sought his advice on securing a record contract. Now head of Denmark Productions, Page had previously enjoyed some mild success in the 1950s as 'Larry Page the Teenage Rage', touring with Cliff Richard, and performing at the Royal Albert Hall and on TV shows such as *Thank Your Lucky Stars*. Ray describes Page as 'tall, but not quite as tall as Wace and Collins. He had fair to blond hair and his face was framed by a pair of thick black-rimmed spectacles, which gave him the look of a cartoon character' (Ray Davies, 1994: 97). More importantly, Page had strong musical instincts and because his background was closer to the Davies brothers he was seen as 'a down-to-earth guy, [who] we felt we could trust' (Ray Davies, 1994: 97). In addition to his connections to Kassner, Page provided the complement they needed to their management team: 'Larry had the wheeler-dealer, street-wise expertise to find his way into meetings with record companies, and Robert and Grenville had the society contacts to get that person into any club in Mayfair' (Ray Davies, 1994: 97).

It was Page who hired record producer Shel Talmy (1937–), who helped the band audition for record contracts and who produced their work through 1967's *Something Else by The Kinks*. While Talmy would also enjoy success producing the Who, Page earned acclaim managing/producing the Troggs. (When he heard the Who's 'I Can't Explain' and the Troggs' 'Wild Thing', Ray felt a sense of betrayal, that the Kinks' sound had been stolen by these other bands.) While Page was the one member of the management team who accompanied the band on their disastrous North American tour, he abandoned them in California, shortly after he signed a deal for Sonny and Cher to record Ray's 'I Go To Sleep'. While Page accompanied the band on a 1966 European tour, his days with the Kinks were numbered; a lawsuit was waged against Page and Kassner, and when the appeal was resolved in June 1967, Page no longer retained his 10 per cent interest in the Kinks.

Eddie Kassner (1920–1996) was a music publisher of Jewish Viennese descent; while he narrowly escaped the Nazis, his parents died in Auschwitz. In London, Kassner married and in 1944 established the music publishing company Edward Kassner Music Co. Ltd. He wrote songs under the name Eddie Cassen, but his career took off in the 1950s when he decided to focus on music publishing, acquiring the rights to songs recorded by Frank Sinatra, Perry Como, Nat King Cole and others. For $250, he bought the rights to 'Rock Around the Clock', often cited as the biggest-selling vinyl rock 'n' roll single of all time. When Page funnelled Ray's songs to Kassner, the latter gained 10 per cent of the Kinks' income as well as the lucrative royalty fees of being the songs' publisher. Kassner played an odd role during the disastrous US tour as he was not officially with the band, but according to Ray, quietly followed the band across the country (Ray Davies, 1994: 244). Once the band reached Los Angeles, Kassner took on a more visible role; however, his prime aim was to sell Ray's songs to artists such as Peggy Lee, who, like Sonny and Cher, opted to record 'I Go To Sleep'.

Ray has described Kassner as short and stocky, with 'thick, horn-rimmed spectacles' and 'dark soulless eyes' who bore the 'look of a man who had been exposed to extreme suffering and whose soul had been punished to the point where all feelings for the rest of humanity had been squeezed out of him' (Ray Davies, 1994: 180). In the *Denmark Productions Ltd* v. *Boscobel Productions Ltd* lawsuit, Kassner's separate claim to continue as Ray's publisher dragged on until 1970 when Davies finally agreed to settle out of court for a reported

£30,000 (the equivalent of £650,000 in 2012); while the lawsuit was active, the songwriting royalties from 1965 onward were held in escrow, and so it was not until 1970 that Ray actually received royalties for most of his hit songs of the 1960s (Hasted, 2013: 159–160).

Allen Klein (1931–2009) was a New York-based businessman whose tough persona and aggressive negotiation tactics had earned him a reputation for his ability 'to extricate artists from unsatisfactory contractual arrangements' (Ray Davies, 1994: 299). In 1965, Klein successfully renegotiated the Rolling Stones' contract with Decca Records (to one far better than the Beatles had), and so Wace, Collins, and Davies rightly believed he was the man they needed in their battle with Page, Kassner, and Pye Records. While Klein managed the Rolling Stones from 1965 to 1970 and the Beatles from 1969 through their dissolution, he also eventually earned the wrath of these same artists who came to see their deals with Klein as disproportionately enriching Klein himself. Ultimately, the Rolling Stones were involved in litigation with Klein for well over a decade. While a controversial figure, Klein was instrumental in establishing higher industry standards for compensating recording artists and his lasting influence is summed up in the title of Fred Goodman's 2015 biography: *Allen Klein: The Man Who Bailed Out the Beatles, Made the Stones, and Transformed Rock & Roll*. (Klein's business partner was Marty Machat; the character is listed in the Hampstead programme, but is omitted from the London programme. However, Machat, transformed to a female character, does appear in both productions and is performed by the actress who plays Mrs Davies.)

Brian Sommerville (1932–) is another member of the early management team. The former publicist for the Beatles who joined the Kinks team in 1964 just as 'You Really Got Me' was released, Sommerville has a couple of brief unacknowledged appearances in *Sunny Afternoon*. Though the event did not make it into *Sunny Afternoon*, Sommerville is part of a legendary early Kinks story. One day during his spring 1966 nervous breakdown, Ray rolled up his money in a sock and ran six miles down to Sommerville's Denmark Street office. Bursting into the office, Ray threw a punch but missed, with Sommerville ducking and hitting his head. Being 'attacked by a madman', Sommerville summoned the police, and in Ray's own words, 'what followed was a Keystone-cops-style chase around the small alleyways surrounding Denmark Street. [With me evading the police until] I ended up in Eddie Kassner's office' (Ray Davies, 1994: 280). Ray seeking refuge with Kassner was ironic in that Ray had recently broken with Kassner and signed with another music publisher, the basis for the prolonged legal dispute that would torment Ray for the rest of the decade.

Sunny Afternoon's creative team

While musicals are the most commercial side of live theatre, they are still a hit or miss proposition. A majority of scripts never make it to production, and even those that do often fail to make money. Beyond simply the idea, it takes the right creative team to develop the concept and manifest it in theatrical terms. While *Sunny Afternoon* has been a critical and commercial success, it is not the typical, glitzy West End musical. The production's approach is rooted in the theatrical sensibilities of the creative team. Notably, the writer, director, and designer of *Sunny Afternoon* were all novices at musical theatre; however, their work in straight theatre provided the right combination of experiences to tell the story of a band whose personalities and story mesh with the kind of characters and situations often found in drama.

Joe Penhall (1967–) began his career as a journalist. While his one-act play *Wild Turkey* (1993) premiered at the London New Play Festival, it was the Royal Court Theatre's production of his first full-length play *Some Voices* (1994) that marked Penhall's emergence. Winning the John Whiting Award (for showing a new and distinctive development in dramatic writing with particular relevance to contemporary society), *Some Voices* offers a razor-sharp, yet sensitive, portrayal of the challenges that people with mental illness face as they try to re-integrate into society. His follow-up *Pale Horse* (1995), another Royal Court production, focuses on a bar keeper dealing with the sudden death of his wife; it won the Thames Television (Pearson's) Award. Penhall cemented his status as a major playwright via the National Theatre's production of *Blue/Orange* (2000), another foray into the realm of mental illness. With expertly crafted dialogue and vivid characterization, *Blue/Orange* probes mental health, medical ethics, and race as it pits two white National Health doctors against each other as they dispute the best way to treat a young black man who is likely schizophrenic. *Blue/Orange* won the *Evening Standard*, Olivier, and Critics' Circle Awards for Best New Play; a 2016 Young Vic revival also won critical acclaim. Penhall has also written for television and film, most notably the screenplay for Cormac McCarthy's *The Road* (2009) as well as extensive uncredited work on *The Last King of Scotland* (2006).

While *Sunny Afternoon* is Penhall's only musical, his connection to the Kinks goes back to the early 1990s. Penhall recalls: 'When I first started writing plays, The Kinks were a big source of inspiration for me. I would listen to the lyrics of songs, not the hits, but the buried songs on albums, and kind of mine them for inspiration' (Cuthbertson, 2015). As a twenty-three-year-old reporter for the *Hammersmith Guardian*, Penhall interviewed Ray and later saw the Kinks 'in their dying moments' at the Royal Albert Hall. He recalls:

> Even then I had an idea I wanted to work with him. Later I went to see him play a solo show at the Bloomsbury Theatre and left him a copy of my play *Pale Horse*, and a letter suggesting we collaborate. This was in 1995.
>
> (Mortimer, 2014)

In 2011, producer Sonia Friedman made that wish a reality when she suggested Penhall to Davies. In addition, Penhall notes that while writing *Some Voices*,

> I was listening to The Kinks a lot, and I can see the influence in the play. It's clear to see if you read that play, some of themes, the tone, certain preoccupations share a tiny fleck of DNA with this.
>
> (Mortimer, 2014)

Notably, the three main male characters are named Ray, Dave, and Pete, and the schizophrenic Ray 'was based on a gifted musician friend who I'd always imagined had gone mad under the weight of his own pure genius' (Penhall, 1998: *x*).

Penhall was also important because he had a strong enough personality to manage the sometimes tempestuous Davies. Penhall relates that their initial 'bromance' and strong collaboration 'rotted into a cancerous feud' when Davies became increasingly involved in writing the show's dialogue. Davies would suggest line changes based on his own 'unauthorized autobiography' X-Ray; after Penhall made the changes, Davies accused Penhall of plagiarism and sought a writing credit. Ultimately, Penhall maintained full credit for the book, with Davies getting a story credit. Fortunately, the show's success healed the rift between the two men (Hemley, 2016).

Edward Hall (1966–) is the son of famed director Sir Peter Hall. While directing Shakespearean productions at the Watermill Theatre in the 1990s, Hall created Propeller Theatre, an all-male Shakespeare company. One of their most acclaimed productions was *Rose Rage*, Hall's ambitious 2002 adaptation of the three parts of Shakespeare's *Henry VI*; it earned critical accolades during its West End run as well as on Broadway and at the Chicago Shakespeare Theater. Never one to shy away from large-scale projects, in 2000, Hall joined his father to co-direct the three-part, ten-hour production of *Tantalus*, John Barton's epic look at the Trojan War. An Associate of both the National Theatre and the Old Vic, Hall became Artistic Director of the Hampstead Theatre in 2010. There he has continued its tradition of developing new work, with *Sunny Afternoon* being its first musical. Hall's work for film and television includes two episodes of *Downton Abbey*.

Miriam Buether was born in Germany, studying costume design in Hamburg and stage design in London. In 2010, she won the *Evening Standard* Award for Best Designer for work on *Sucker Punch* (Royal Court) and *Earthquakes in London* (National Theatre), for which she also earned an Olivier nomination for set design. For *Sucker Punch*, the main theatre at the Royal Court (usually in a proscenium/ end stage configuration) was redesigned as an alley theatre with a boxing ring in the middle. with audiences on two sides. Likewise, *Earthquakes in London* employed a similarly effective immersive environment as part of the audience stood or sat on stools situated on the central floor of the performance area while a long s-shaped runway snaked through the audience. Additional audience members sat in regular seats along the two sides of the alley while the smaller ends featured proscenium-like stages for select scenes. For both productions, the actor–audience arrangement created a sense of immediacy and engagement, traits she also achieved when she and Hall collaborated on Hampstead's 2012 premiere of *Chariots of Fire*; for that production the entire theatre was transformed into an Olympic stadium, giving audiences the sense/experience of being fans in the Olympic stands. These designs suggest why she was an ideal choice for *Sunny Afternoon* as the area behind the proscenium evoked a recording studio while the centre walkway and side ramps fostered interaction between the band and the audience when in a concert-like setting. Other major designs include the Young Vic's 2012 production of *Wild Swans* for which she earned an Olivier nomination for Best Set Design and won the Critics' Circle Theatre Award for Best Designer.

2

Act One

Sunny Afternoon is both a bio-drama and a jukebox musical. Each of those aspects creates its own artistic challenges. While a documentary strives to stick to the facts, by its nature a bio-drama necessitates taking certain liberties; in many ways the goal is to present the *truth* of the situation as opposed to strictly the facts. The result is a necessary compression and/or conflation of events and people to capture the essence of the lives and situations. The added challenge of a jukebox musical is that the bio-drama needs to be told through the music of an individual group. Within these parameters, writer Joe Penhall expertly made distinct choices as to which aspects of Ray Davies' original story and song catalogue to use to best craft a show that would provide an entertaining account of the Kinks' early years. The following provides an analysis of the structure, story, songs, and content of Act One. In the process, the approach considers: why did Penhall select these events and songs? How do they reveal character, theme, and the core story of the Kinks? It also tries to answer: how accurate is the portrayal?

At the outset, it should be noted that the script is unpublished and was not made available by Penhall's agent; thus quoted dialogue is my own paraphrase based on multiple viewings. In addition, when needing to distinguish between fiction and history, the band member's first name indicates the stage character while the surname denotes the historical person.

Sunny Afternoon opens with the band members milling about onstage, as if warming up before a recording session or concert. The observant audience member will notice that the drum kit reads 'The Ravens'. The subsequent appearance of a tall lead singer named Robert 'Bobby' Wace, and a crowd of partygoers in tuxedos and ballroom gowns may make the casual Kinks fan wonder if they wandered into the wrong theatre. Wace's crooning rendition of 'You Still Want Me' adds to the seeming dissonance between expectation and presentation. It is only when a young, impulsive, long-haired guitarist (Dave Davies) bellows out a 'Fuck this', and the musicians launch into the driving drums and crunching guitar riffs of 'I Gotta Move' that the audience seems to enter the realm of the early Kinks.

This opening vignette is not strictly factual, but it effectively captures the essence of some early gigs when Ray, Dave, Pete, and drummer served as the backing band for Wace on the debutante circuit. In reality, the band was known as the Boll Weevils when Wace fronted them (and sang Buddy Holly songs rather than the Kinks first single 'You Still Want Me'). Likewise, while Ray was initially a hesitant lead singer, on the actual night that Wace was booed off stage, it was Ray, not Dave, who stepped in as lead singer. On the other hand, the subsequent dialogue where Collins champions the energy generated by the young Dave allows for an apt expression of the important role Dave played in stirring up excitement (particularly with females) among their early fans.

The scene proceeds to convey the essence of how Wace and Collins came to be the band's managers. The class divide between management and band is evident in Wace's 'they have a certain unwashed *je ne sais quoi*' and Collins' 'they're raw, scruffy working-class oiks'. Likewise, Collins' statement 'Exclusivity is out, inclusiveness is in' suggests the ultimate role that pop music would play in shaking up the social structure of 1960s England.

While telling the essential story, Penhall also seeks moments where simple lines can provide a quick, bold stroke of characterization. When Ray starts to strum and sing 'A Well Respected Man', Dave observes that Ray 'thinks in song'. In a *Daily Mail* article that Ray penned in conjunction with the West End opening he wrote:

> I've always expressed my feelings best in song. There is a key line in the musical, 'I think in song', and it's true. If I met someone and had coffee with them, I would immediately start thinking up a tune about them.
>
> (Ray Davies, 2014)

In a similar vein, the subsequent scene's jam session between Ray and Dave playing 'Just Can't Go To Sleep' suggests the bond the brothers formed over music, and the initial harmony they shared before the infamous acrimony settled in as the dominant narrative of their sibling relationship. This scene also includes a seemingly innocuous line that Ray has trouble sleeping because he cannot switch off his mind, a fact that will resonate more strongly in Act Two.

While the scene provides some family context (with four sisters and mum), it ultimately leads to one of the pivotal moments in the band's history: the creation of 'You Really

Got Me'. Typical of their process, Ray plays the chords on piano, and then Dave translates to guitar. Penhall has fun with the scene as Dave's early guitar riffs (acoustic, electric, and then double amplified electric) are all 'too civilized' with 'not enough violence'. The crucial moment occurs when Dave takes his famous little green amplifier and slices up the speaker cone; in Penhall's version, Ray then also stabs it with a knitting needle. This addition of Ray's co-assault on the amplifier drew the wrath of Halstead, whose *Independent* review referenced the moment as a 'blasphemous rewriting of The Kinks' foundation myth' (Halstead, 2014); Dave himself took to a message board declaring: 'I ALONE CREATED THIS SOUND … I am just flabbergasted and shocked at the depth of [Ray's] selfish desire to take credit for everything [including] my guitar sound' (Dave Davies, 2014). On stage, the slicing of the amplifier leads to the legendary crackling, fuzz guitar sound that changed rock 'n' roll history.

Just as 'You Really Got Me' is the song that made the Kinks, Penhall uses the moment to segue the story back to the business side as a new song requires a publisher. The jaunty 'Denmark Street' (complete with a short tap-dance number) provides a concise account of the music publishing industry in the mid-1960s, with Davies unloading his venom by having Kassner sing: 'I hate your music and your hair is too long/ But I'll sign you up because I'd hate to be wrong.' (Historically, Page and Kassner always disputed Ray's unflattering portrayal of them in songs such as 'Denmark Street', arguing that they actually liked the music, that it was more than just business.) While meeting Larry Page and Eddie Kassner, Wace and Collins casually note that Mick [Avory] is the new drummer. From this moment on, the four principal band members and four principal managers are now all part of the stage story. While the band is wary of adding more people to the management team, Page glibly states: 'You can never have too many managers.' While there is much quibbling over the relative financial splits (with it all clearly stacked in management's favour), the reality of the situation (and the seeds of the future legal/financial dispute) is summed up in Page's line: 'You just write the songs, Ray. We'll take care of the business end.' Ultimately, the scene closes with a rendition of 'A Well Respected Man', with both Wace and Collins thinking the song is about himself and thus taking up verses of the song; for Penhall, it is the apt use of a beloved Kinks hit that also serves to characterize the founding duo of the management team.

Despite the fact that the contract is weighted heavily in management's favour, the band is ready to sign; however, the one sticking point (which would later prove to be historically significant) is that Dave is still a minor, and thus a parent needs to sign for him. This allows Penhall to move the action back to the Davies home, a chance to convey the family's working-class roots. Mr Davies reveals that that the family has always rented, never being able to afford a home. Never having even seen £500, Mr Davies is bewildered that a home in Muswell Hill costs £3500, with his delivery indicating that this is a ridiculously astronomical price (which always evokes a laugh from an audience in today's much inflated housing market). The power of the scene comes when Mr Davies starts singing 'Dead End Street'. Davies provides a brilliant arrangement as Mr Davies' lament 'There's crack up in the ceiling/ And the kitchen sink is leaking' is later joined by Mrs Davies' plaintive 'And my feet are nearly frozen/ Boil the tea and put some toast on'; throughout choral lines such as 'What are we living for?' are picked up by the six Davies children (with the historical touch of Gwen on banjo). While the lyrics evoke the stress of working-class life, the closing section is a triumphant musical celebration with the trombones offering hints of a New Orleans-style jazz parade and the siblings' vigorous singing and dancing providing a sense of the joyous Saturday night music parties at the Davies household.

Penhall uses the post-song dialogue to convey the family's working-class pride, while also providing some family background such as Mr Davies playing banjo in the music hall and sister Rene giving Ray his first guitar. The parents also discuss their two sons, identifying Dave as a strong, masculine male and Ray as more introspective and sensitive. (The line is that Ray 'boils at a different temperature'.) Mrs Davies believes that Rene was the one who knew what made Ray tick and that Ray's mission as a songwriter is about something more than money or fame. Mrs Davies also strongly rebuts Kassner, telling him that he does not understand Ray, but that one day he will, one way or another. Ultimately, Kassner appeals to Mr and Mrs Davies as both a businessman and as a father, that by signing the contract the boys will have opportunities and material things the parents never did. Just before signing Mr Davies asks if management is getting the usual 10 per cent commission; the answer is 'yes', but it is 10 per cent for each of the four managers, plus a cut to the booking agent. Though Kassner asserts there is nothing 'insidious' about the contract, Mr Davies is appalled that over 40 per cent will go to management. Despite the terms, Ray is anxious for his dad to sign and when Page says that a new band called the Who pays their managers 20 per cent each, Dave also urges his father's signature before management changes its mind. Then in a theatrical flourish, Ray sings a few lyrics from a haunting reprise of 'Dead End Street' which gives way to the signing of the contract and the trombone flourishes of the joyous 'Dead End Street' celebration.

With the contract signed, the action shifts to management crafting a marketing plan for the band; in this case it means a trip to Carnaby Street for stage outfits. As the band dress in their legendary green hunting jackets, Pete asks 'how do we look?' and Page responds 'kinky'.

In *X-Ray* (Ray Davies, 1994: 102–104), Davies provides an account of how Page devised the band's name and look, and Penhall again distills a longer story into its essence as onstage Page suddenly declares that 'Kinks' would be a good name for the band: it is short, weird, would stand out at the bottom of the bill, and would attract the curiosity of girls. In keeping with the historical record, Page proceeds to suggest they add whips, leather, and riding boots, some of the iconic marketing images from the band's early days. In management's estimation, the band members are not good looking enough and so some type of gimmick is needed to sell them.

When Ray argues they need songs more than a gimmick, it is suggested he write a song about Dave, because girls love Dave. While admitting that songwriting does not quite work that way, the script engages in a little hagiography as Dave declares that songs just come to Ray, and that Ray 'is a victim of his own genius'. As if proving the point, the line is quickly followed by the opening chords to 'Dedicated Follower of Fashion'. Penhall adds a nice comic bit as Ray does a double-take and declares 'what the fuck is that?' as he discovers Dave decked out in a feather boa. Dave's donning of a purple floppy hat is another historical detail (see Dave Davies, 1996: 89) that adds to the theatrical presentation of the hit single. Notably, in *Sunny Afternoon*, while Ray sings most of the lead vocals, Dave is given select lines, lyrics such as 'this pleasure-seeking individual always looks his best' and 'the one thing he loves is flattery'; these arrangement choices suggest the lines are meant to characterize the young Dave.

Another part of preparing the band for public appearances draws on another aspect of Kinks lore: Ray's front teeth. As happened in early 1964, Ray is taken to a dentist so that the gap in his front teeth can be fixed by removing the two front teeth and replacing them with caps. Penhall uses the moment to draw a distinction between Davies and management. Page says that replacing his teeth is a 'small sacrifice to make for fame', but Ray counters that his teeth 'might be ugly, but at least they're real'. In the ensuing debate, Page asserts: 'Do you want to hold on to your integrity or do you want to be a star?' It is Dave who notes that it is 'a tricky question', and the scene ends with the question verbally unanswered, but with the front teeth gap remaining and the action transitioning to an early interview with the band.

The interview allows Penhall to provide historical background on the other band members. Pete reveals that he and Ray were friends at art school, that they grew up together in Fortis Green, and that they have known each other since they were ten years old. In turn, Mick notes that he used to sell paraffin out of a van and that he turned down a job with the Rolling Stones because he 'couldn't see no future in it'. Dave's contribution to the interview is that he 'likes hard drugs [at the time it was pills and hash, with harder drugs in later years] and wearing women's clothes'. The interview closes with a reiteration of management's position that complicated is good, that complicated sells.

This is roughly the halfway point of Act One, and the action moves to a critical point in the Kinks' history: the recording of 'You Really Got Me'. The stage presentation somewhat obscures what was at stake; since the first two singles flopped, the band was down to its last shot, the final recording in their contract. If the third single failed, the Kinks may have faded into history as a simple footnote, one of the many bands that recorded songs, only to disappear. (In *X-Ray*, Davies provides a detailed account (146–151) of how he successfully fought for a second recording session to get the single re-recorded.) On the other hand, Penhall's presentation captures the differences of opinion regarding 'You Really Got Me' and how it should sound. As Dave plays the opening chords, Page (serving as the stage amalgamation of himself and producer Shel Talmy) stops him, declaring the sound 'Too raw, too uncivilized'. A second attempt is called 'Too violent. They'll never play it on the radio like that.' Page proceeds to put reverb on it and suggests slowing it down and adding some overdubs. This is management's attempt at making it sound commercial, but Ray is understandably horrified, declaring: 'You can't do this to me.' He proceeds to state, 'This is the best song I've ever written. It may be the only hit song I ever write.' Ultimately, Ray fights for the song to be recorded the way he hears it in his head.

As he often does, Penhall uses the closing line as the segue into the next scene, and here it is 'You Really Got Me' as Ray hears it in his head and as performed on *Top of the Pops* (complete with go-go dancers) as the new #1 hit song. While its energetic performance serves as an Act One highlight, Penhall expertly uses the aftermath for more personal introspection. Mr Davies expresses his immense pride in Ray (see Ray Davies, 1994: 172), but rather than revel in fame, Ray reveals his fears, his reluctance to be a pop star: 'I don't think I can do this. I don't want to do this. I've changed my mind.' It is Mrs Davies who counsels: 'Don't tear yourself down with doubts, son. There are plenty of people who will do that for you.' In turn, Mr Davies urges Ray to never back down, to never give up, and 'to never forget who you are'. As his parents walk away, Ray's plaintive singing of a piano-ballad rendition of 'This Time Tomorrow' suggests his acceptance of his future as a rock star, a fact echoed by the screaming crowd that segues 'This Time Tomorrow' into a raucous 'Set Me Free' positioned as part of a Sheffield concert.

The choice of 'Set Me Free' and its staging aptly introduce the next critical plot point: the relationship between Ray and Rasa, who indeed met after a concert in Sheffield when he was twenty and she was eighteen. During the song, various girls (would-be groupies) approach the band and Ray, but he has no interest in any of them; however, when Rasa enters, she clearly catches Ray's eye, and so when the song ends, Ray strikes up conversation. While Ray fishes for compliments, Rasa's repeated reply is that it was all right. Rather than throw herself at Ray, Rasa proceeds cautiously, with Ray prying out the historical background of Rasa being a Lithuanian refugee now living in Bradford. (In a seemingly historical embellishment, Rasa also references Big Bill Broonzy, the American blues legend who was one of Ray and Dave's early influences.) In the midst of Ray and Rasa's conversation, Dave is pursued across stage by three females; in contrast, Ray desires a monogamous relationship (which is the main thrust of 'Set Me Free').

The contrast between the brothers is further heightened back at the hotel, Dave is now wearing a dress as he frolics with the three women and sings 'Till the End of the Day'. Notably while Ray sang 'Set Me Free' with its lines 'If I can't have you to myself/ I don't need nobody else', it is Dave who sings 'Baby, I feel good/ From the moment I arise … We do as we please, yeah/ From morning, till the end of the day.' The thumping rock anthem underscores the ensuing stage mayhem, an evocation of the Kinks' reputation for trashing hotels. The staging choices subtly reveal character, with Pete on a Mod scooter, Wace and Collins playing cricket, and both band and management indulging in groupies, while Ray is off to the side with Rasa. The scene culminates with Dave, in a pink dress and leather jacket, swinging from a chandelier and then taking an axe to the hotel desk.

The stunning theatricality of the scene was noted by many reviewers, and audiences may rightly wonder if Penhall and Hall have engaged in some embellishing of the facts. Did that event actually happen? The answer of 'yes and no' highlights the expert way the show conflates separate events to convey an essential truth. There are many instances of the young Dave wearing women's clothing, but there is also an account of Dave, dressed in armour (thus, the seemingly odd inclusion of the suit of armour being brought on stage during the scene), swinging from a chandelier in a Scottish castle (see Ray Davies, 1994: 176). Later on that same tour Dave, along with a member of Gerry and the Pacemakers, took an axe to a hotel reception desk when they could not get into a bar that was closed because it was 2:00 in the morning (Dave Davies, 1996: 59). Via the conflation of these separate events, Penhall quickly and memorably demonstrates the flamboyant, sexually ambiguous, and volatile personality of the young 'Dave the Rave'.

Dave's wild partying is contrasted by Ray's courting of Rasa, who needs to go home because she has school in the morning. When Ray is willing to leave the tour's party atmosphere to go back to Bradford with Rasa, she questions 'What kind of pop star are you?' Indeed, the transition to the next scene highlights how the brothers use their musical fame to pursue different interests: Dave drinks champagne and pops Purple Hearts (amphetamines) with his three groupies while the religious-sounding music aurally references Rasa being at convent school.

The subdued scene between Ray and Rasa offers some of Ray's most personal revelations. Indeed, the first lines convey some often overlooked background. Ray says: 'We're not really brothers. We are, but Dave doesn't see it that way. Because I abandoned him when I went to live with my sister Rosie after Rene died.' (In *Kink*, Dave notes that he was close with his nephews Michael and Bobby, but that '[our cousin] Terry and Ray were probably more brother-like in their relation than Ray and I' (Dave Davies, 1996: 12).) Then in his most personal revelation Ray tells the story of his sister Rene giving him his first guitar for his thirteenth birthday, the same day she died. As Rene played piano, she started softly singing a lullaby, with Ray struggling to play along on guitar. Ray describes Rene's song as an unfamiliar, probably self-created, tune that was strange, bewitching, and beguiling, a song that cast a spell over him. He adds: 'To this day I can't recall how it went. But every time I sit down to try to write a song, I hope it's going to be that one.' This hypnotic story gives way to 'This Strange Effect', now sung as a duet between the new lovers, with them each declaring: 'You've got this strange effect on me/ And I like it.' In the midst of their expression of mutual affection, Ray adds: 'You really can sing; you should sing on our records', thus opening the door to Rasa's future as a backing vocalist on some of the early Kinks records.

With the romantic subplot firmly established, the action shifts back to the business side with Kassner revealing that 'You Really Got Me' is a world-wide success. Now to be 'wealthier than you ever imagined', all Ray has to do is write another hit song. While Ray sits down with a typewriter, Kassner has an extended monologue that reveals his personal backstory, often trying to draw a parallel between himself and Ray. (Details are capped by the phrase: 'Just like you.') The break between personal identification occurs when Kassner reveals how the Nazis drove him out of Austria, with his family being sent to Auschwitz, and Kassner escaping to London. Kassner's compelling personal narrative is soon swallowed by the aural magic of Ray's typewriter (accompanied by piano) pounding out the familiar opening notes to 'All Day and All of the Night'. Recognizing that Ray has indeed written another hit, Kassner triumphantly tells Ray: 'I am going to make you immortal. I'm going to make you my redemption.'

In the following scene (a conflation and rearrangement of events covered in *X-Ray* (Ray Davies, 1994: 182–184)), Ray and Rasa meet in London. While Ray thinks this will be just another happy get-together, Rasa utters a string of significant revelations: she was expelled from school; she spent time in the hospital after fainting; and, most importantly, she thinks she may have had a miscarriage. Before a shocked Ray can respond, Rasa adds that her parents are strict Catholics and they did not leave Lithuania to spend the rest of their lives in shame. Rather than discuss what they might do, she suggests, 'Dave could be your best man'. Ray's response – 'Dave. In a church. With a load of bridesmaids. Are you mad?' – provides some comic relief, but does not change the fact that Rasa is pregnant and Ray is expected to marry her. Ray tries to dodge her by saying that he cannot get married now because he is about to go on tour with Gerry and the Pacemakers. In real life, Davies knew Rasa was pregnant and had agreed to marry her before most of the other events happened. On the other hand, Ray's joke about Dave references the fact that during the reception, when Dave was supposed to be giving the best man toast, he was upstairs having sex with the maid of honour (Dave Davies, 1996: 48).

The transitional newsflash makes it clear that the wedding will indeed happen. Rather than joy or a personal reaction, management expresses concern over how, in a market driven by young female fans, this is bad for business. Publicist Brian Sommerville laments: 'Why wasn't I even consulted about this? It's all over the press. It will ruin everything.' Sommerville notes that when he worked for the Beatles, for years they concealed John Lennon having a wife and child because 'The Beatles are professionals.' In addition to the cold side of business, Dave is also worried about Ray's marriage: 'I dropped out of school to do this, and if we break up now, mum is going to kill me', a line that unwittingly reveals his immaturity. Then in one of the great ironies, Dave says, 'Why can't you keep it in your pants, Ray?' Ray's reply, 'You can talk. You and Brian Jones,' alludes to Dave's bisexuality. (In *Kink*, Dave discusses the mutual, but unconsummated, sexual fantasy he and Brian Jones shared for each other (Dave Davies, 1996: 51–52); on the other hand, Dave readily acknowledges having a sexual relationship with *Ready Steady Go* host Michael Aldred (54), among other men and countless women.) The scene escalates until Ray says, 'You've had everybody', and then mockingly adds 'I'm Dave the Rave', at which point Dave tries to attack Ray, but is restrained by Pete. This is the first stage depiction of the legendary infighting that plagued the brothers and the band.

Ray and Rasa's wedding, in December 1964, was indeed a shock to the pop world, and the use of an almost-choral version of 'Stop Your Sobbing' plays with the notion that the news of Ray's impending marriage greatly upset many female fans. *Sunny Afternoon*'s use of a girl running into the wedding pleading 'Don't do it, Ray' echoes the reality of what was written on the signs of many female concertgoers (see Ray Davies, 1994:183). In a compressed nod to the fast-paced commercial nature of the times, the brief joy of the wedding is quickly followed by Page's insistence that now, even though Rasa is about to give birth, is the time to tour America.

In addition to the impending child, Ray resists going to America, in part because he is afraid of getting shot. Rather than an anachronistic nod to the gunshot wound Davies suffered in New Orleans in 2004, it reflected his view: 'America. Guns. Seeing Kennedy killed on TV a few years before had made me think that the whole continent was full of assassins, serial-killers, and Mob-style corporations' (Ray Davies, 1994:239). Page's glib assessment that pop stars are not important enough to get shot rings with the post-modern irony of John Lennon's later murder. More significantly, Page insists that the Kinks need to crack America; until then they will only be a second-tier band. In contrast, Ray stresses that the band needs to evolve musically, that more than just entertainment, people want music that is meaningful, that expresses their lives. Just when it seems that Ray will get his way ('Whatever you say, Ray. You're the talent'), the tables are quickly turned as Page follows with, 'Smoking or non-smoking', indicating that ultimately management will win.

The subsequent brief rendition of 'This is Where I Belong' evokes Ray's growing contentment as a family man, and his distaste for the touring that takes him away from his beloved England. The ensuing phone montage offers a quick snapshot of the other band members. Mick's frustration over the lack of recording and touring does not fit in the hectic spring of

1965 (but does reflect the feelings of spring 1966 when Ray's breakdown following the American tour significantly reduced the band's activities); on the other hand Mick's complaint that Dave keeps stealing his birds might reference the fact that Mick and Dave were sharing a house, a party den where the bedrooms were nicknamed 'Whore's Hovel' and 'Spunker's Squalor' (Dave Davies, 1996: 54). Then, in a complaint that would be more apt for 1967, Dave wants to write more songs and have more creative input. He even threatens to write a solo album (which following 'Death of a Clown' was often rumoured), with Ray's putdown being that an EP may be possible, but not a full album. For his part, Pete wants to leave the band, citing his isolation from the other band members, a fact that would increase in the ensuing years. While the facts of the phone calls are anachronistic, dramatically they serve the important purpose of highlighting the increasing tension and fragmentation within the band.

Indeed, the next scene depicts one of the most infamous events in early Kinks history: the onstage brawl at a Cardiff concert on 19 May 1965. Mick and Dave are engaged in a bitter row as they set up their gear for the show. In the midst of their fighting, Ray receives a phone call with news of his daughter's birth (which was actually 23 May), emblematic of Ray's new position as a family man versus the band's aggressive, partying image as well as representing the fact that touring and the band's business side allowed no significant pause for personal lives. The ensuing medley captures the energy and volatility of a Kinks show circa 1965, with an apt choice of 'Where Have All the Good Times Gone' as the lead offering, a comment on the state of the band. During the song Dave and Mick resume their fight and the song breaks down. With a switch to 'All Day and All of the Night' there is hope that the fight is over, but as a young, undisciplined band under great pressure, it is only a brief respite before the blow-up. After Dave messes with Mick's drum set, Mick has had enough and proceeds to violently strike Dave over the head with a drum pedal. Worried that he may have killed him, Mick flees, pursued by police. Playing both his bass and Mick's drums, Pete gallantly tries to make the show proceed. Ray is incredulous, finally declaring: 'Only a madman would tour America with this group, a bloody madman.' This closing scene and curtain line serve as apt foreshadowing for Act Two's ensuing disastrous American tour.

3

Act Two

Act Two opens with the band embarking on one of the pivotal events of their early career: the disastrous American tour that resulted in their four-year ban from the United States. The events of the tour (travelling from 17 June 1965 until 11 July 1965) take up one-third of the second act's playing time, revealing the confluence of circumstances that resulted in the hard-to-fathom ban that prevented the Kinks from capitalizing on the American market the way the Rolling Stones, the Who and others did in the British Invasion of the mid-to-late 1960s. From a historical perspective, it is worth remembering that when the tour commenced Dave was only eighteen years old, Ray was about to turn twenty-one (with his first child less than a month old), and it was the first time the band had played together under the rigours of a tour since the previous month's brawl at Cardiff. The tour exposed the band's youth, instability, and lack of management.

On stage, the initial impression of the tour stands in stark contrast to its results. As the lights rise, Ray sings a jaunty rendition of 'This Time Tomorrow' as the centre catwalk represents an airplane as the band members take their seats, drink, and flirt with the flight attendants. If it were just a holiday, the light-hearted party atmosphere of the plane ride may have been apropos for the young band members' experience; however, once on the ground, it is clear that this a business trip. Though he does not know the band's correct name, Gregory Piven introduces himself as their American Federation of TV and Radio Artists representative in New York City. He quickly asks them to sign a release and pay their dues in advance. There is instant confusion as the band are not members of the union; however, Piven asserts that they have visas and one of the conditions of those visas is having agreed to join the union. Piven notes that if they want to appear on television, they must join the union; it is the only way to protect them from non-union members. Pete cleverly unravels Piven's argument: since the Kinks are non-union members, 'it would appear that you are protecting us from ourselves'. Losing that point, Piven then posits that since the Kinks play 'essentially Negro music', how is it fair for a British act to play in America which already has its own Negroes that are entitled to the work? While Piven's argument resonates with contemporary debates over immigration and employment opportunities, it is left unresolved as there are numerous other complications facing the band.

On the business side, the band is clearly out of its depth, and so they summon the one manager who accompanied them: Larry Page. Prancing around in a cowboy hat, Page is portrayed as a man on vacation and not as someone looking out for the band. The tour's complexities are quickly revealed as in addition to Piven, the American Federation of Musicians is looking to collect dues from the band's performance the previous night and the Teamsters transportation union (which was strongly influenced by organized crime) are owed some money as well. Soon a Mob-like man welcomes the band on behalf of Mr Sinatra, but with the proviso that Mr Sinatra urges them to take care of Jimmy from the Teamsters as well as their driver. The power of the unions, as well as the Mob influence of the 1960s, are on full display, and not even Page understands enough to be able to provide the assistance they need.

In addition to the business complexities, the tour had its share of British Invasion moments as soon the stage is engulfed with screaming female fans, with the band protected by a squad of armed police officers. The rebellious, outsider status of the Kinks is revealed in the banter among the police officers: 'I've never seen hair like that before'; 'They make the Rolling Stones look like US Marines'; 'Did anyone ever tell you your brother looks like your sister?'; and 'Are you a Beatle or a girl?'. Whereas the other bands had well-oiled PR machines and experienced management to guide them, the Kinks were four young non-conformists left to fend for themselves in a world that did not always make sense and which was not always welcoming to them. Indeed, their driver in Illinois wonders 'what kind of a motherfucking name is [the Kinks]', has a car phone, and, most importantly, wields a pistol that terrifies the band members.

The thug-like driver presented on stage depicts a person Ray remembers meeting in Illinois (see Ray Davies, 1994: 240–244). While that encounter was unsettling, meticulous Kinks researcher Doug Hinman reports a more startling fact, discovered years later: The man who organized the Kinks' hastily added concert in Springfield, Illinois was future serial killer John Wayne Gacy, then the Vice President of the local Jaycees (a civic, service organization that provides leadership training for young adults), who promoted the event with proceeds benefiting the Jaycees Scholarship Fund. While Hinman doubts the Kinks had a direct encounter with Gacy, Quaife asserts that the local promoter (i.e. Gacy) drove them around all day and that the band went to Gacy's house after the concert, drinking until 4 a.m., with Gacy being upset that the band, particularly Dave, would not stay longer (Hinman, 2004: 58; Hasted, 2013: 50–51; Jovanovic, 2013: 96).

While Gacy's involvement with the Kinks tour is shocking, Penhall wisely steers clear of it, as it would distract from the main narrative, which is now focused on the general struggles of the tour. The subsequent restaurant scene between Ray and Larry Page provides a snapshot of how poorly it is going. In a partly fictional statement that captures the essence of the situation, Ray says both a Boston concert and *The Ed Sullivan Show* got cancelled, and that failure to pay a withholding tax in Philadelphia nearly landed them in jail. (In reality, those were not the cancellations, and it was Page who was briefly jailed for failing to pay the obscure tax.) While there was indeed a suspicious power outage during the Kinks' performance in Chicago, Page asserts that everything is now under control and they can look forward to playing the Hollywood Bowl with Sonny and Cher. Then in one of the factual oddities of the tour, Kassner appears, revealing that he has been following Ray across the country.

The ensuing dialogue reveals the fissure that has been developing, pitting Page and Kassner against Wace and Collins, as the respective teams battle for Ray's loyalties. When Ray says that all the touring is tearing the band apart, driving them insane, Kassner says not to worry because they are insured. To protect his own royalty flow, Kassner did indeed take out a life insurance policy on Davies (see Ray Davies, 1994: 278), but then in a dramatic embellishment that strikes to the core of the situation Kassner proceeds to say: 'I own 51 per cent of the music, which means that technically I own 51 per cent of … you.' Since the imbalance of the power structure is unsettling, Kassner tries another approach, asserting how proud his parents are and how proud his sister Rene would be. The personal appeal impacts Ray as he again recounts Rene's death, now adding that she died 'doing something she loved, it must mean something'. Kassner asserts that it is a sign, and that 'This [being a rock star] is your destiny!' The close of the scene suggests that Page and Kassner are hopeful that they have won Ray over, that he will let them be his guides.

After a two-minute drum solo (an homage to Brubeck drummer Joe Morello) the focus briefly shifts to the status of the other band members. Mick has fulfilled a dream by seeing jazz great Dave Brubeck (and meeting Morello) at the Hollywood Bowl. In contrast, Pete laments that it is no longer fun and that he misses his family. (In reality, after the tour Mick and Pete spent additional time in Los Angeles, and so this seems to be a dramatic foreshadowing of Quaife's eventual desire to leave the band.) For his part, Dave enters wearing a sequinned dress, noting that somewhere there is a woman wearing his underpants. Pete sums up the precarious nature of the band: 'The trouble with us is, we need each other, we just don't like each other.'

Since *Sunny Afternoon* is told from Ray's perspective, the personal effects of the tour focus on him and his family. When Ray calls Rasa, the audience is reminded that he has an infant daughter at home, with Rasa barely sleeping as she carries the responsibility of caring for the child. In the ensuing conversation, it is clear that despite the band's forthcoming performance with a star-studded line-up at the Hollywood Bowl, Ray is miserable. He laments that, fed up with them, Page has returned to England, but only after selling one of Ray's songs to Sonny and Cher. (In reality, after Ray barricaded himself in a hotel room and refused to perform, Page met Ray's difficult demand that the visa-less, Lithuanian-born Rasa be flown over; Page stayed for a few songs of the Hollywood Bowl performance before exiting unannounced, leaving them to finish the tour alone.) Instead of enjoying the rock 'n' roll life, Ray, in a motif that would resurface on the Kinks' 1986 album *Think Visual*, compares life in the music industry to working in a factory, only without the job security. Regarding the tour so far, from Ray's perspective, perhaps the one saving grace is that no one has tried to murder anyone yet.

The scene gives way to a beautiful rendition of 'Sitting in My Hotel', Davies' 1972 ballad about the alienation and artifice of life on the road (despite the luxuries of being chauffeured around like a star). After the song, Rasa asks a fundamental question: 'This is what you've always wanted, so why can't you be happy?' In an answer that contrasts Ray Davies from probably all the other rock stars of the era, he simply says: 'I'm homesick.' He expounds: 'Homesickness is a real sickness, and it rots you to the core. And the only cure for it is to go home.' Ray's one comfort is for Rasa to tell him how much she misses him. This results in a lovely rendition of 'I Go to Sleep', a poignant ballad about separated lovers and the very song that Page had sold to Sonny and Cher.

A short instrumental of 'Who'll Be the Next in Line' is used as a transition to the next scene: the fateful encounter with a union official backstage in a North Hollywood television studio. The scene's opening is fictionalized as the official asks who sings the backing vocals, wondering whether they contract out or sing like a girl. Ray's revelation that it is his wife Rasa, leads to the line, rich in post-modern irony: 'I can tell you Paul McCartney would never put his wife on a record.' More importantly they want to know if Rasa is in the union. (For their *Shindig!* performance that was lip-synched, the band had to re-record a song with American musicians to cover the parts that had been performed by non-union musicians (Hasted, 2013: 53).) While Rasa was never actually part of the dispute with the union officials, her family's Lithuanian background raises the spectre of whether anyone in the band is a Communist. Dave proudly declares: 'We're working-class socialists from Muswell Hill!' As tensions continue to boil, the union official insists they pay their dues and go home. Fed up, Ray tears up the paperwork and proclaims: 'Sorry, we've paid enough dues for one tour.' As the union official declares 'You just killed yourself', the band launches into their defiant anthem 'I'm Not Like Everybody Else'. The song closes with Ray and the union official each lightly placing their hands on the other. When the union official declares, 'Did you see that? He just assaulted me?', Dave strides forward saying 'That's not an assault. This is an assault', and violently head-butts him. While there are various accounts of what happened backstage that day (see Ray Davies, 1994: 251; Hinman, 2004: 60; and Jovanovic, 2013: 98), most include Ray punching someone, but none include Dave's head-butt. For his part Dave says:

> I never knew why we were really banned until I [recently] discovered it was Ray who got us banned. [*Sunny Afternoon* uses my character] for dramatic emphasis, but it was not true. I never hit any officials. I wasn't there so I don't know what really happened.
>
> (Dave Davies, 2014)

In an apt telescoping of time, in the aftermath of the American tour, the stage action quietly jumps from summer 1965 to spring 1966 when another monumental Kinks event occurred: Ray's psychological breakdown. Historically, in early March 1966, after a quick European tour, Ray was diagnosed with physical and nervous exhaustion; bizarrely, while Ray was bedridden, the band was sent back to Europe for another short tour, but with Mick Grace of the Cockneys impersonating Ray while Dave was moved to lead vocalist. Rather than recuperate, Ray's condition initially worsened as on 17 March, he arose from bed and ran six miles to central London where he attempted to assault their publicist Brian Sommerville. The stage action essentially picks up after that moment when Ray is again bedridden, now at the depths of his physical and psychological malaise.

Looking bedraggled and listless, Ray lies in bed as he receives a series of visitors. Penhall uses the guests for personal revelation and social commentary, as well as light-hearted humour. Mrs Davies laments that someone was bound to get hurt, while Mr Davies opines the irony that 'the only socialist band gets brought down by the unions'. As a concerned mother Mrs Davies urges Ray not to take things so personally, to have some perspective, while Mr Davies feels somehow responsible. The underlying subtext reveals a working-class family thrust into the limelight, but lacking the personal and social acumen to navigate all the demands of pop fame.

Ray has not spoken a word during his parents' visit, and so it is up to the second guest, Rasa, to provide the necessary exposition of Ray's exhaustion, of his having slept for nearly a week. Rather than just focus on Ray, Penhall uses the scene to convey the reality that Rasa ultimately faced, the reality often faced by other spouses of famous people: namely, that everyone else gets the best of Ray, and so that by the time he is home with her, there is nothing left. Rather than engage in a conversation, Ray lapses into song, a poignant rendition of 'Too Much on My Mind', a composition Davies wrote during his breakdown. Whereas Davies often writes songs from a character's point of view, as an insomniac with a paranoid streak, these lyrics are starkly personal: 'My thoughts just weigh me down/ And drag me to the ground/ And shake my head till there's no more life in me./ It's ruining my brain/ I'll never be the same/ My poor demented mind is slowly going'. The magnificent arrangement turns into a beautiful duet before splitting into parallel songs with Ray's mental anguish counterpointed by Rasa singing 'Tired of Waiting for You'. For the intensely private Davies, the scene was difficult but necessary. In a *Daily Mail* article, Davies recounts how seeing the masterful performance by John Dagleish was

> hard to take. I thought: 'Christ, what have I done?' I am such a secretive person, and I was showing one of the most difficult times in my life. But it had to be done to tell the complete story.
>
> (Ray Davies, 2014)

After this emotional, personally affective scene, Dave saunters in jauntily singing 'Dedicated Follower of Fashion'. The selection may reflect the fact that during Ray's breakdown the song was steadily climbing the singles chart (hitting #4) as well as the fact that strangers singing the lyrics into Ray's face while he walked the streets may have played a role in his breakdown (see Ray Davies, 1994: 279). Dave is joined by Wace and Collins who try to cheer Ray up and assert that pop stars like Ray are the new aristocracy. Wanting nothing to do with 'Swinging London', Ray finally speaks, lashing out at the fashion world and pop culture as distractions from the poverty-stricken people stuck in the breadlines. He also argues that 'Exclusivity is back in', a reversal from Wace and Collins' first act pronouncement. When Ray laments the Kinks being the only band ever banned from America, Wace articulates a central aspect of the Kinks' existence, the fact that the Kinks sometimes refused to play the game. When Dave argues that Ray cares more about winning than playing the game, Wace notes that business is not about single winners and losers, it is about both sides winning. As the conflict escalates, Wace posits that 'the Kinks are fundamentally unmanageable'. To provide some comic relief, Penhall inserts a fictitious phone call from Brian Sommerville urging Ray to get out of bed and do some press, adding: 'You wouldn't catch John Lennon loafing about in bed with his wife.' The audience's post-modern laugh over the 1969 Bed-ins for Peace staged by Lennon and Yoko Ono serves as an apt break-point to move to another topic.

After brief references to members of the Beatles and Stones, the conversation flips to the other major event occurring at the time: the relative lack of royalties/income the band members were receiving in comparison to their success and the lawsuit it inspired. Historically, in the months between the American tour and Ray's breakdown, Davies instructed Wace and Collins to hire a lawyer to sever business ties with Page and Kassner. On stage, Ray's lament over their financial situation inspires a rendition of 'The Moneygoround', a bouncy, musical revue-style song about the music industry that directly names Wace, Collins, and Page as taking more than their fair share of the money. The lyrics provide a quick encapsulation of the legal situation, and the song's close segues straight into Ray serving Kassner with a legal writ. For

Kassner, it is the saddest day of his life, a day on which a man he loved like a son, a man whom he made rich (and who made him rich) betrayed him. For his part, Page accuses Ray of being self-serving. In contrast, Ray argues that his responsibility is to his music. In reality, it was about the money, as well as the control. ('The Moneygoround' makes oblique reference to *Kinky Music*, the 1965 album of instrumental versions of early Kinks songs performed by the Larry Page Orchestra, a project Ray detested.)

While recovering from his breakdown, Davies wrote one of his most iconic songs, the title track 'Sunny Afternoon'. (That such a joyous-sounding song could emerge from one of his darkest moments stands as one of the great testaments to Davies' genius.) On stage, a clever snap of Ray's fingers to the beat of 'Sunny Afternoon' segues the action to the 13 May 1966 recording of the song. While 'Sunny Afternoon' would ultimately be one of their greatest successes, the stage shows the increasing conflict that percolated among the band during recording sessions as Ray exerted increasing control. In particular as Ray insists on another take, Pete is tired of the incessant takes and is frustrated by his lack of creative input. In a fictitious bit (that was true with 'You Really Got Me', but not with 'Sunny Afternoon'), Wace says 'We can't afford to go again. This is your last throw of the dice. The record company has agreed to give you one more shot at a new record, but we can't spend all day in an expensive studio.' Penhall's inversion of the circumstances (from what was true in July 1964 but not May 1966) serves to refocus the legal issues as Wace's statement provokes Ray's question: 'We've sold millions of records, so where's all the money?' Wace counters with the reality that Davies faced: as long as the legal case was unresolved, all songwriting royalties were placed in escrow. To cap the argument, Ray asserts that if they record the song his way and put it out at the start of the summer 'it will be the biggest hit of 1966. They'll be singing it from the rooftops … and England will win the World Cup final!' It is yet another moment where Penhall's knowledge of history allows him to score points with an appreciative audience.

Understanding Ray's concern over his royalties being placed in escrow, Wace suggests, provided they have the stomach for it, a bold course of action. Wace's ominous 'I know a man, who knows a man' serves as an apt introduction for Allen Klein, the legendary New York accountant known for renegotiating bad music contracts. The ensuing scene depicts Klein as a hard-nosed businessman and his lawyer Machat as a sharp legal mind. Machat articulates the essential legal issues including Dave being a minor when the contract was signed and Page's undisclosed relationship with Kassner being a conflict of interest. Machat also adds the historical fact that the Beatles originally had an even worse royalty rate than the Kinks did. Beyond the dense legalese, Penhall adds some interesting characterization. When Ray says that he feels like an idiot for signing the original contract, the brash Klein asserts:

> No, you feel guilt … All victims feel guilt. Reality is, you're just as fricking ambitious as I am. You just don't know it yet. That makes you corruptible. So don't come to me like Little Orphan Annie with all this phony British modesty.

Notably, Ray does not argue against any of this assessment. While Ray tries to maintain that he just wants the money he deserves, Klein counters that what Ray really wants is revenge. In addition to resolving their contract issues and getting the copyrights back, Klein also promises to fix the issues with the American musicians unions so that the Kinks 'will be playing Madison Square Garden when the Beatles are in their graves'. The one moment where Ray asserts himself is when Klein wants some American songs, whereas Ray proudly says that he writes about England.

The ensuing scene is a second-act highlight as the band performing their #1 hit 'Sunny Afternoon' is intertwined with an announcer calling the World Cup final between England and West Germany. On that historic day, the band members watched the extra-time finale until the very end, even though it meant being seriously late for a concert in Exeter. That same day, after victory was secured, the joyous English crowd at Wembley Stadium gleefully sang 'Sunny Afternoon', thereby making the Kinks song England's unofficial anthem for the glorious World Cup summer of 1966. On stage, the magic of the moment is capped by confetti cascading down on stage and audience alike as a reprise of the song, with Union Jacks waving, mimics the victory parade and country-wide celebration.

On stage, the joy of victory is short-lived as in the ensuing scene Pete informs the band he is quitting. While Ray praises him and tries to convince him to stay, Pete recalls Ray's critique of the bum notes he played and the way he feels taken for granted, as the outsider who does not fit in with the band. Even Ray's joke that Mick doesn't hate Pete, he hates Dave falls on deaf ears. Pete recoils at the pressure and the instability of the band, harkening back to the early days when they were kids rehearsing at the youth centre in Muswell Hill. Though not directly stated, Pete's speech highlights the degree to which the band's infighting sapped much of the original joy, the days when they would do anything to have the opportunity to play. Saying that he is sorry to disappoint his old friend Ray, Pete launches into a poignant rendition of 'A Rock 'n' Roll Fantasy'. Again Davies' arrangement expertly assigns different lyrics to different characters so that the song is partially a dialogue, with Ray taking the second verse: 'You say you want out/ Want to start anew, throw in your hand/ Break up the band, start a new life, be a new man/ But for all we know, we might still have to go.' But Quaife gets the last word, with a plaintive a cappella delivery of the song's closing line: 'Don't want to spend my life living in a rock 'n' roll fantasy.'

To push the show to its conclusion, Davies and Penhall must compress time and conflate history. Just after Pete resigns, Wace and Collins announce that Klein wants to represent the band and will get them a six-album advance. Despite any past conflicts, Ray wants Wace and Collins to remain the band's representatives, but the managers maintain that the time has come and that it is a bad idea to mix with other classes, that ultimately people revert to type. As they prepare to gracefully resign, they have no regrets and depart with a heartfelt a cappella rendition of 'Days' and its sentiment: 'Thank you for the days/ Those endless days, those sacred days you gave me.' On stage, it is a crowd-pleasing send-off for their mismatched managers. (Historically, in 1966, Klein did secure a renegotiated five-year deal with Pye Records, but it was not until late 1971 that the band signed their six-album contract (with advances) from RCA, and that is when Wace and Collins departed.)

With Wace and Collins gone, Ray and Dave must decide whether or not to sign with Klein. In a scene that mixes business dynamics with sibling relationships, Dave urges Ray to listen to him for a change; they went to Klein for help, and so they should sign with him. However, Ray is worried that history will repeat itself, that a new deal with Klein will eventually lead to a similar set of legal issues. Dave notes the great change that has occurred; whereas it was once about the band and the music, it is now about ownership and court cases. The other great change is Dave's evolving maturation, his starting to view life as an adult, someone who strives for marriage, a home, and a family, just like a normal person. When Ray questions whether Dave wants to be like Ray, Dave comically replies 'I wouldn't go that far.' Interestingly, Ray's follow-up is an admission that sometimes he wants to be like Dave. Kinks fans may recognize the scene as a dramatic embodiment of their 1967 song 'Two Sisters', an allegory in which the domestic sister (Ray) longs to be like the party sister (Dave), only to eventually decide that the children make the domestic life more rewarding. Notably, in the scene, it is Dave who stresses family, of wanting to see more of Ray, Rasa, and their daughter. In some ways the scene foreshadows the eventual reality that Dave would ultimately (at least partially) forego his persona of 'Dave the Rave' and would be more of the family man, taking an active role in the lives of his four sons.

The scene's comic touch of Dave thinking he is old at age twenty-three ultimately prompts a moving rendition of 'A Long Way From Home'. Here Ray sings directly to Dave telling him: 'You've come a long way from the runny-nosed, scruffy kid I knew/.../I can remember the little things that always made you smile.' It soon turns into a dialogue with each brother singing: 'Now you think you're wiser because you're older and you think/ That money buys everything.' After each brother asserts 'You don't know me', the song erupts into a passionate exchange that closes with each brother singing to the other 'Yes, you're still a long way from home.' Then to underscore the song's sibling sentiments, Edward Hall's staging aptly portrays the love-hate dynamics as Dave swats off Ray's arm before the brothers embrace in a full hug. The scene's final action is Ray signing the contract as Dave had asked. (The scene's reference to Dave being twenty-three is another second-act anachronism. Dave was indeed twenty-three when Ray wrote 'A Long Way from Home' and was another year older when the RCA contract was signed; however, the stage time coincides with spring 1967 and the creation of 'Waterloo Sunset', a period when Ray was twenty-two and Dave was twenty.)

The intense scene between the brothers gives way to Pete's return. While one critic viewed the bassist's quick return as almost *Spinal Tap*-like (Marlowe, 2014), it actually hews close to history. Injured in a car accident in the summer of 1966, Quaife was temporarily replaced by bassist John Dalton. Though physically recovered, Quaife quit the band in September 1966, only to return that November (Hasted, 2013: 83). More importantly for the stage story, Pete returns because he is interested in playing the 'walking bass line' that Ray had previously described: as soon becomes clear, it is the unmistakable intro to the iconic 'Waterloo Sunset'. Regarding the ensuing scene, Davies wrote:

> I wanted the show to end on a high. The highly romanticised final scene in the musical shows how – despite our differences and disagreements – the band came together one more time to record my new song Waterloo Sunset: my ode to London, my hometown.
>
> (Ray Davies, 2014: 62)

Strikingly, Davies was afraid the band might laugh at the lyrics, and so both the music and backing vocals were recorded with no one else knowing the song's content (see Ray Davies, 1994: 338). Rather than laugh, audiences have been captivated and moved for over fifty years, highlighted by its inclusion in the closing ceremony of the 2012 London Olympics.

'Waterloo Sunset' is a blend of expressionistic and impressionistic songwriting, a way of 'painting with sound' (Ray Davies, 1994: 339). On stage, Ray refuses to reveal the lyrics, saying: 'It's not about the words, it's about the atmosphere.' He proceeds to say that the song conveys his feeling of home, of London, of us, of lost and found, of being alone but together. He concludes: 'The songs are about us, all of us; they always have been.' He adds that he doesn't like to talk about the songs, that doing so might spoil them. As they continue developing the song's sound, Rasa describes it as beautiful. When she says it makes her want to cry, Ray proclaims: 'If you don't cry, you're probably dead. Yeah, stick that on the poster.' Then the band launches into a full-version of 'Waterloo Sunset' that provides the mesmerizing high that Davies sought.

While the recording and performance of 'Waterloo Sunset' is ostensibly the closing scene, Davies and Penhall have a clever conceit that shifts the musical into a concert-like setting. As he would do in live Kinks concerts, near the end of 'Waterloo Sunset', Ray asks the audience to acknowledge 'David Russell Davies on guitar'. This foreshadows the concert motif as the band soon exit the stage to loud applause; however, a concert calls for an encore and *Sunny Afternoon* delivers it in spades. Before the audience's applause dies out, Klein enters and bellows out 'Welcome to Madison Square Garden!' This proclamation fulfils his earlier claim and serves as a twofold postscript as it suggests the 1969 lifting of their ban in America as well as their future success as an arena rock band.

The jump forward from 1967 also allows for a concert-like performance of one of the Kinks' biggest and most enduring hits: 1970's 'Lola'. With Klein's introduction of 'The Kinks!', the band return to the stage and launch into a crowd-pleasing medley of 'Lola', 'All Day and All of the Night', 'You Really Got Me', more 'Lola', and then some closing power chords of 'You Really Got Me'. As with a concert, the band encourage the audience to get on its feet, clap, and sing along. Whereas standing ovations are the norm in American theatre, they are exceedingly rare in London, but the Davies–Penhall encore concert conceit ends with the audience on its feet, singing and clapping with the euphoric energy of a vintage Kinks concert. For long-suffering Kinks fans who have clamoured for a reunion for nearly twenty years, this amped-up, dynamic encore is the closest thing there is. Indeed, in the absence of a reunion, *Sunny Afternoon*'s appearance in 2014 served as an apt tribute to the fiftieth anniversary of one of the great rock bands of all time.

Appendix A

Sunny Afternoon fact sheet

Premier production: Hampstead Theatre

Previews beginning 14 April 2014
Official opening 1 May 2014
Limited run until 24 May 2014

Cast in alphabetical order

Sister/Company	Carly Anderson
Mr Davies/Allen Klein/Company	Phillip Bird
Eddie Kassner/Company	Ben Caplan
Ray Davies	John Dagleish
Pete Quaife	Ned Derrington
Rasa/Company	Lillie Flynn
Sister/Company/Dance Captain	Emily Goodenough
Mrs Davies/Machat/Company	Helen Hobson
Larry Page/Company	Vince Leigh
Dave Davies	George Maguire
Sister/Company	Amy Ross
Mick Avory	Adam Sopp
Gregory Piven/Company	Marvin Springer

Robert Wace/Company	Dominic Tighe
Grenville Collins/Company	Tam Williams
Guitarist	Pete Friesen

Creative team

Music and Lyrics	Ray Davies
Book	Joe Penhall
Original Story	Ray Davies
Director	Edward Hall
Designer	Miriam Buether
Lighting Designer	Rick Fisher
Sound Designer	Matt McKenzie
Musical Supervisor and Director	Elliott Ware
Choreographer	Adam Cooper

West End production: Harold Pinter Theatre

Previews beginning 4 October 2014
Official opening 28 October 2014
Closing 29 October 2016
Twenty-eight-city UK tour: August 2016 through May 2017

West End cast and creative

Same as Hampstead except:

Gregory Piven	Ashley Campbell
Mrs Davies/Marsha	Elizabeth Hill

Sister(s) now specified:

Gwen	Carly Anderson
Peggy	Emily Goodenough
Joyce	Amy Ross

Awards won

2015 Laurence Olivier Awards
  Best New Musical
  Outstanding Achievement in Music (Ray Davies)
  Best Actor in a Musical (John Dagleish)
  Best Actor in a Supporting Role in a Musical (George Maguire)

Additional award nominations

2015 Olivier for Best Sound Design (Matt McKenzie)
2014 Evening Standard Award nominations
  Emerging Talent Award (John Dagleish)
  Ned Sherrin Award for Best Musical
2014 Whatsonstage.com Awards
  Best New Musical
  Best Supporting Actor in a Musical (George Maguire)

Appendix B

The songs of *Sunny Afternoon*

The original cast recording of *Sunny Afternoon* includes twenty-nine tracks, twenty-eight of which appear in the show. The following provides background information on each song. Andrew Hickey's 2012 book *Preservation: The Kinks' Music 1964–1974*, offers an excellent resource, including musical analysis, on every Kinks song from their first decade. Ray Davies' 1994 'unauthorized autobiography' *X-Ray* provides additional insight. All songs written by Ray Davies; lead vocals by Ray on all songs except 'I'm Not Like Everybody Else'. The UK chart rankings are based on *Record Retailer*; the US ones are based on *Billboard*. (For a fuller listing of worldwide ranking sources, please see KindaKinks.net.)

Act One

1. **You Still Want Me** (1964): This was the band's second single (following their cover of 'Long Tall Sally'); it failed to chart. In *X-Ray*, Ray expressed relief at its being a flop:

Although it was a sweet enough pop song with a good beat, the only thing worse than its eventual failure was the possibility of it being such a big hit that we would be forced to perform it every night for the rest of our career.

(Ray Davies, 1994: 117)

2. **I Gotta Move** (1964)/**You Really Got Me**: 'I Gotta Move' was the B-side to 'All Day and All of the Night' and represents the riff and blues-based songs the band played in their early years. Here, 'You Really Got Me' is performed by an a cappella chorus, similar to the arrangement found on 2009's *The Kinks Choral Collection*.

3. **Just Can't Go to Sleep** (1964): The song appears on their debut album *Kinks*. Hickey asserts that it 'sounds like an early attempt at the hook for "Stop your Sobbing"' (13).

4. **Denmark Street** (1970): Recorded for *Lola versus Powerman and the Moneygoround, Part I*, an album in which nearly half the songs are about the music industry, the song's title references the fact that Denmark Street was the place in London where the majority of UK music publishers were located. It glibly argues that publishers do not care if they like the music, they only care about making money.

5. **A Well Respected Man** (1965): The song appears on the UK chart-topping EP *Kwyet Kinks*; as a single it reached #13 in the US. Hickey sees it as a song that transformed the Kinks: 'Davies learned the secret of writing melodies for his limited vocal range' and significantly improved his lyrics, writing 'a biting, cynical, pen-portrait of a member of the upper-middle (or lower-upper) classes, full of a joy at wordplay we've never seen from him before' (37). In

addition, while Davies has 'never been the most rangy or versatile of vocalists, here he learns that he's good at taking on personas and singing in different characters' (37).

6. **Dead End Street** (1966): The follow-up to 'Sunny Afternoon', this single reached #5 in the UK, but only #73 in the US. The grim social commentary on the debt-ridden lower classes still rings true today. Long before MTV, they shot a promo film featuring the bandmates as undertakers with a corpse that ultimately leaps from its coffin initiating a Keystone Kops-like chase. Deeming it in poor taste, the BBC refused to air the video.

7. **Dedicated Follower of Fashion** (1966): This single reached #4 in the UK and #36 in the US. Like its predecessor 'A Well Respected Man', this song is another sharp essay in social satire. Written after a brawl with a fashion designer at a Christmas party hosted by Davies, the song skewers London's fashionistas and conformity. A direct jab at the purveyors of Carnaby Street, then the most famous fashion-shopping street in London (beloved by Dave Davies as well as Mods of the era), the song offers a witty mix of humour and venom.

8. **You Really Got Me** (1964): Following two failed singles, 'You Really Got Me' was the band's last chance; if it failed, that would be the end of their recording contract. The demo had been recorded during their first session, but the song was not considered commercially viable. Proving popular at concerts, the song was recorded; however, unsatisfied with its studio sound, Ray successfully fought for a last-ditch re-recording, trying to capture the raw power of the song when played live. This final version, with its loud, distorted guitar and screaming, lustful vocals, epitomized teenage sexual tension; it shot to

#1 in the UK and #7 in the US. Hickey articulates the song's historical impact: 'Angry, frustrated, raunchy, this is the precise moment when rock – as opposed to rock 'n' roll – was invented' (15).

9. **This Time Tomorrow/Set Me Free** (1965): Their fourth single following their breakthrough, 'Set Me Free' was another hit, reaching #9 in the UK and #23 in the US. Though pleasing the Kinks' management team, in Davies' own words, the formulaic attempt to write a generic, commercial pop song 'made me feel like a whore' (Ray Davies, 1994: 233). On the other hand, the song's lyric stands in stark contrast to the brewing sexual revolution as the singer longs for a monogamous relationship.

10. **Till the End of the Day** (1965): The song reached #8 in the UK, but only made #50 in the US. Appearing on their third album *Kink Kontroversy*, Hickey calls it 'the last of the band's generic pop singles. After this, all the rest of the band's hits would be music that only they could have done' (46).

11. **This Strange Effect** (1965): Davies wrote the song for Dave Berry and patterned it after Berry's previous hit 'The Crying Game'. For Berry, the song reached #37 in the UK charts and was a #1 hit in Belgium and the Netherlands. The Kinks recorded it for the BBC radio show *Top of the Pops*. It appears as a bonus track on the reissue of *Kinda Kinks*.

12. **Stop Your Sobbing** (1964): The song appears on their debut album *Kinks*; it was the first to feature Rasa on backing vocals. In 1979, the Pretenders covered the song as their first single, and it reached #34 in the UK.

13. **This is Where I Belong** (1967): This was the B-side to 'Mr. Pleasant' (which itself soon became the B-side

to 'Autumn Almanac'). Lyrically, the song expresses contentment in a love relationship.

14. **Where Have All the Good Times Gone** (1965)/ **All Day and All of the Night**: Appearing on *Kink Kontroversy* and as the B-side to 'Till the End of the Day', 'Good Times' is hailed by Hickey as 'an absolute masterpiece' that may be 'the first post-modern pop song' (48). A rock song about depression and nostalgia, Hickey champions the lyrics:

> This tension – this longing for a past which is acknowledged as being mythical and never having really existed, while also trying to push forward in progressive directions that wouldn't have been possible in the past, and self-reflexively commenting on both these tendencies – would become the most important and unique aspect of Ray Davies' songwriting.
>
> (48–49)

Act Two

15. **This Time Tomorrow** (1970): From *Lola versus Powerman*, this song evokes the transient nature of a touring rock band. Neither brother was fond of flying, but as they tried to re-conquer America, they, as the song says, frequently found themselves: 'on a spaceship somewhere sailing across an empty sea'.

16. **Maximum Consumption** (1972): A studio track from *Everybody's in Showbiz*, the song reflects an obsession with American food. Hickey observes:

> After becoming detached from his home country and the people around him, the protagonist of the song

[seemingly Davies himself] is starting to think of his body, too, as something other, something that's moving around independently of his wishes, a machine that requires food and sex.

(173)

17. **Sitting in My Hotel** (1972): Another studio track from *Everybody's in Showbiz*, this piano-based ballad 'sounds like an experiment in writing musical theatre' (Hickey 175). The lyrics strike to the heart of Davies' sense of alienation while on the road.

18. **I Go To Sleep** (1965): Never released by the Kinks, the demo (which appears as a bonus track on the reissue of *Kinda Kinks*) was used to sell the song to other artists, as both Cher and Peggy Lee recorded it in 1965. Of the more than twenty cover versions, the best known is the Pretenders' 1981 version which reached #7 in the UK.

19. **I'm Not Like Everybody Else** (1966): Sung by Dave, this song (originally intended for the Animals) was the B-side to 'Sunny Afternoon'. Its strident sense of individualism made it an unofficial anthem for the band. Detractors note the irony that the song was later used in advertising campaigns by corporate giants such as IBM.

20. **Too Much on My Mind** (1966)**/Tired of Waiting for You** (1965): Written in the aftermath of his March 1966 nervous breakdown, the former appears on *Face to Face* and aptly captures the mindset, and unwanted thoughts, of someone suffering from severe anxiety. The original includes Rasa's high harmonies accompanying Davies' lead vocal.

Though only a small portion of the song appears in the show, 'Tired of Waiting for You' was one of the band's biggest hits, #1 in the UK and #6 in the US, their highest ranking there. Written before 'All Day and All of the Night', it was held back so that the more similar-sounding song served as the follow-up to 'You Really Got Me'.

21. **The Moneygoround** (1970): Part of *Lola versus Powerman*, this song takes direct shot at the Kinks management team as Wace, Collins, and Page are all called out by name for their profiteering. Hickey sums up this Noel Coward-esque song: 'Funny, clever, and entertaining, and complaining about a real problem without being angsty' (140).

22. **Sunny Afternoon** (1966): One of the band's biggest hits (#1 in the UK and #14 in the US), the song, originally entitled 'The Tax Man's Taken All My Dough', was composed during Davies' recovery from a nervous breakdown when his therapeutic routine was:

> The sunny days of early spring 1966 consisted of getting up, writing a song, playing with my daughter, lunch in the back garden, the afternoon resting in a dark room, then back in the sun, more song-writing and bed. Bliss.
>
> (Ray Davies, 1994: 283)

23. **A Rock 'n' Roll Fantasy** (1978): From a very different era than the other songs in the show, this track from *Misfits* reached #30 in the US. While the musical uses the song to express Pete Quaife's flirtation with leaving the band, in his 2013 Kinks biography Nick Hasted asserts that Davies told a writer that it 'was a very personal song about Dave and I' (222) and the band's near break-up in 1977. In Dave's words:

It's a lovely song about being disillusioned with the rock business and wanting to give it up, and meeting a fan who reminds you of the reasons why you wanted to do it in the first place and rekindles the urge to keep going.

(Dave Davies, 1996: 187)

24. **Days** (1968): Written to commemorate the end of an emotional affair, Davies retrospectively asserts that the song was also a subconscious prediction of the original band's break-up (Ray Davies, 1994: 359–360). Indeed, 'Days' was the last single released with the original line-up, and it reached #12 in the UK, but failed to chart in the US.

25. **A Long Way From Home** (1970): A more personal, self-reflective song from *Lola versus Powerman*, 'A Long Way From Home' is often thought to be addressed to Dave as well as to Ray himself. Hickey asserts:

Whether this is Ray singing to Dave, or Ray taking on the persona of someone from Muswell Hill talking to Ray, it's fair to say that the critique in the song summed up how both men felt at the time.

(141)

26. **Waterloo Sunset** (1967): Ray Davies' performance of 'Waterloo Sunset' at the closing ceremony of the 2012 London Olympics signifies the degree to which this classic has come to be regarded as arguably the greatest song about London, an unofficial anthem for the city. The song hit #2 in the UK, but in the most shocking example of the effect of the ban, 'Waterloo Sunset' failed to chart in the US.

27. **Lola** (1970): The story of a romantic encounter with a transvestite or transgendered woman, 'Lola' stands as a quintessential Kinks song. Accounts of the song's origins vary: 'At various times, Ray Davies has said the song is about Avory, about his own (apparently non-sexual) meeting with Candy Darling, and about the Kinks' manager Robert Wace going home with a trans woman, too drunk to care' (Hickey 138). While the subject matter was striking, ironically, the biggest controversy stemmed from the use of the words 'Coca-Cola' as a BBC ban on brand names necessitated a 6000 mile round trip for Davies to overdub the words 'cherry cola'. After the ban from the US and the critically acclaimed, but poor-selling, albums of the late 1960s, 'Lola' marked a return to hit-single status as it reached #2 in the UK and #9 in the US. Likewise, the song remained a centrepiece of Kinks' concerts to the very end.

28. **All Day and All of the Night** (1964)**/You Really Got Me**: The follow-up to 'You Really Got Me', 'All Day and All of the Night' hit #2 in the UK and #7 in the US. While sonically similar to its predecessor, 'All Day and All of the Night' has always been a concert favourite and remains a rock classic.

Bonus track

29. **Look a Little On the Sunnyside** (1972): A studio track from *Everybody's in Showbiz*. Hickey argues that despite the frequent claim of certain Kinks songs being labelled as music hall-like, this song is 'practically the Kinks' only real excursion into a music-hall style' (178),

with the others more in the vein of songs written for comedy revues versus this song's roots in the 'working-class music hall tradition' (178). On the other hand, the song's rather lightweight lyrics are mostly 'about not letting bad reviews of your music get you down' (179).

Bibliography

Clapp, Susannah (2014), [Review of *Sunny Afternoon*], *Observer*, 4 May. Reprinted in *Theatre Record*, Vol. 34, No. 9, 428–429.

Cuthbertson, Debbie (2015), 'Playwright on song with tale of rock legend', *The Age* (Melbourne), 25 April: 40.

Davies, Dave (1996), *Kink: An Autobiography*. London: Boxtree.

Davies, Dave (2014). http://www.npr.org/2014/11/26/366813240/naive-yet-revolutionary-ray-davies-on-50-years-of-the-kinks. Accessed 20 September 2015.

Davies, Ray (1994), *X-Ray: The Unauthorized Autobiography*. London: Penguin Books.

Davies, Ray (2013), *Americana*. New York: Sterling Books.

Davies, Ray (2014). 'Life as a pop star? It's enough to send a chap off his rocker!' *Daily Mail*, 24 October: 62.

Halstead, Nick (2014), [Review of *Sunny Afternoon*], *The Independent*, 3 May. Reprinted in *Theatre Record*, Vol. 34, No. 9, 428.

Hasted, Nick (2013), *The Story of The Kinks: You Really Got Me*. Revised Edition. London: Omnibus Press.

Hemley, Matthew (2016), 'Sunny Afternoon writer recalls 'cancerous feud' with Kinks star Ray Davies', The Stage, 11 July. https://www.thestage.co.uk/news/2016/sunny-afternoon-writer-recalls-cancerous-feud-kinks-star-ray-davies/. Accessed 30 September 2016.

Hemming, Sarah (2014), [Review of *Sunny Afternoon*], *Financial Times*, 3 May. Reprinted in *Theatre Record*, Vol. 34, No. 9, 428.

Hickey, Andrew (2012), *Preservation: The Kinks' Music 1964–1974* (self-published).

Hinman, Doug (2004), *The Kinks: All Day and All of the Night (Day-by-day concerts, recordings, and broadcasts, 1961–1996)*. San Francisco: Backbeat Books.

Hitchings, Henry (2014), [Review of *Sunny Afternoon*], *Evening Standard*, 2 May. Reprinted in *Theatre Record*, Vol. 34, No. 9, 424.

Jovanovic, Rob (2013), *God Save The Kinks: A Biography*. London: Aurum Press.

Letts, Quentin (2014), [Review of *Sunny Afternoon*], *Daily Mail*, 2 May. Reprinted in *Theatre Record*, Vol. 34, No. 9, 427.

Marlowe, Sam (2014), [Review of *Sunny Afternoon*], *The Times*, 30 October. Reprinted in *Theatre Record*, Vol. 34, No. 22, 1088.

Maxwell, Dominic (2014), [Review of *Sunny Afternoon*], *The Times*, 2 May. Reprinted in *Theatre Record*, Vol. 34, No. 9, 427–428.

Mortimer, Will (2014), 'The Will Mortimer Interview: The Hampstead Theatre Literary Manager talks to the Book Writer Joe Penhall.' *Sunny Afternoon* programme. Hampstead Theatre.

Penhall, Joe (1998), *Plays 1*. London: Methuen.

Rogan, Johnny (2015), *Ray Davies: A Complicated Life*. London: Vintage.

Spencer, Charles (2014), [Review of *Sunny Afternoon*], *Daily Telegraph*, 2 May. Reprinted in *Theatre Record*, Vol. 34, No. 9, 427.

Index

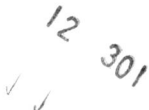

For Product Safety Concerns and Information please contact our EU
representative GPSR@taylorandfrancis.com Taylor & Francis Verlag GmbH,
Kaufingerstraße 24, 80331 München, Germany

Printed and bound by CPI Group (UK) Ltd, Croydon, CR0 4YY
05/12/2025
02013043-0001